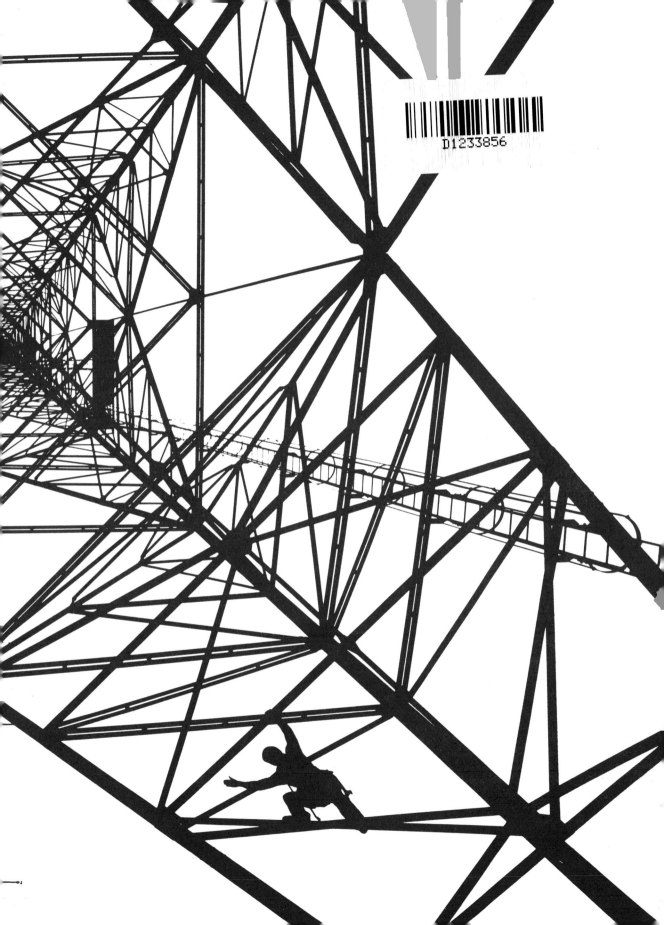

A SKYFUL OF FREEDOM

A Skyful of Freedom

60 YEARS OF THE BBC WORLD SERVICE

Andrew Walker

BROADSIDE BOOKS LIMITED

To Avril (Annie)
Who lived through it

'Tuning in to the BBC is like
sharing a bit of its freedom
as our own'

LISTENER IN BURMA, 1990

'A skyful of lies'

BURMA GOVERNMENT'S
DESCRIPTION OF
BBC BROADCASTS, 1990

First published in Great Britain,
1992, by
Broadside Books Limited
2 Gurney Road
London E15 1SH

ISBN 1874092 03-6

Photographic reproduction of archive material
courtesy of Mahendra Patel at Snappy Snaps,
Basildon, Essex

Printed and bound in Great Britain by the
Bath Press, Avon

Designed by John Meek

*ENDPAPERS: A rigger/mechanic in the 400-feet-high
mast at BBC's Borough Hill transmission station,
near Daventry. The mast, which has given over sixty
years' service, is to be dismantled by the end of 1992.*

Contents

Acknowledgments

RATHER LIKE the British Empire which inspired it, the BBC World Service seems to have grown in a fit of absence of mind. Nobody could have foreseen when it began that it would become a symbol of hope to the people of occupied Europe, nor how it would remain a symbol of hope to those living under later tyrannies. Nobody could have foreseen that it would come to broadcast in 37 languages and claim at least 120 million regular listeners. And nobody could have foreseen that it would pick up various international awards and even be nominated for the Nobel Peace Prize.

After 60 years it is time the story was told. There is already an authoritative history of the first 50 years (*Let Truth be Told,* by Gerard Mansell, a former managing director of the service) but the present book, while containing a good deal of history, also seeks to describe how the service functions to-day and to reflect the considerable impact it has had on events. It is compiled from various sources – the BBC's own archives, published material, including books, pamphlets and press releases, and personal reminiscences, including my own; a good deal of my journalistic career was with the World Service.

I am only too conscious that the story is still incomplete; I was able to talk to some of the great names from the past before they died, but there are many whose reminiscences would have been of enormous interest. Although I have received great help from the BBC in gathering material, it is not an official account, and I have felt free to include some critical comments. Nobody in the organisation asked to 'vet' the manuscript, and the mistakes and misjudgements, are my own.

Thanks are due to a large number of people without whose help and interest the book could never have been written. John Tusa, Managing Director of World Service, allowed me the use of all the facilities of Bush House and interviews with members of the staff. He also submitted to a lengthy interview himself. Without the help of Michael Williams and his assistant, Julia Harris, I should never have been able to talk to half the people I wanted to see. The enthusiasm of Dr. Graham Mytton and Carol Forester of International Broadcasting Research unearthed some fascinating material, including the quotation from the Burmese listener featured on page 5. Catherine Bradley of Broadside Books nurtured the project, gently suggested changes and gave valuable advice. Diana Phillips and Mary Welch were tireless picture researchers and Mary has herself contributed a fascinating history of Bush House, the building. This is particularly timely because the World Service is likely to pack up and go; leaving Bush House as simply a memory. But what a memory! Will it continue to be haunted by the great figures of the past, who beat the Nazi propagandists at their own game, who encouraged people living under Communism to realise there was an alternative and who fought to ensure that the service remained independent of government?

Many people, retired from or still working in the World Service, agreed to be interviewed. I have quoted only some of them, but they all gave me valuable information and insights, and I am grateful to them all. They are: Gordon Adam, Julian Amey, Benny Ammar, Elizabeth Blunt, Mark Brayne, Lawrie Breem, Harold Briley, Derek Brooke-Wavell, Patrick Chambers, Maurice Dalton, Roger Donaghy, Genevieve Eckenstein, Barry Elliott, Paddy Feeney, David Frost, Dorothy Grenfell-Williams, Sheena Harold, Christopher Irwin, Bob Jobbins, Michael Kaye, Simon Long, Alan Macdonald, Callum MacKechnie, Richard Measham, Kate Morgan, Andrew Morton, Ernest Newhouse, Mrs R Obreja, Zeki Okar, Henry Pavlovich, Johan Ramsland, Tom Read, Elizabeth Smith, Gienek Smolar, Gail Styles, Konrad Syrop, Peter Szente, Andrew Taussig, Dennis Thompson, Oung Tun, Mary Wang, Ernest Warburton, Klara Whittall, John Woodward, Elizabeth Wright, Peter Udell, George Yannoulopoulos, Sam Younger. Thanks are also due to Declan Kelly, Richard McCarthy, Mike Popham, Tommy Schwarz and Tamara Stokes for their help.

Without the co-operation of the BBC publicity archive departments, many of the pictures in this book would not have been found. Special thanks are due to Rosemary Sakul-Thongbai, Rosemarie Reid and Susan Stothard at Bush House, and Michaela Southby at White City, for their patient and invaluable help.

Andrew Walker

MAY 1992

Introduction

ESCAPING FROM GHANA had its element of farce, but it was not as difficult as I had feared. Avoiding the airport, where they might have a description of me, I went to the hot, dusty square in the centre of Accra where taxis and buses waited for passengers to all parts of the country. Among the crowds and bustle, horns honking, market women shouting, dogs barking, I should be less obvious.

I found a taxi to the border quickly enough, but I was the last of five passengers and had to squeeze into the back seat between a very large woman and a man who was only slightly smaller. The taxi was a Peugeot station wagon, and it had a flat battery. Whenever the engine stalled, which was frequently, we all had to get out and push until it started again. Eventually the battery gave up altogether, and we had to hang about in a village garage until a new one was fitted. It was hardly the most dignified way for a middle-aged Western journalist to flee the country.

When I reached the border at Togo, the Ghanaian policeman was unexpectedly friendly. This was the bit that had been worrying me. Would he ask me to step into another room to hold me for questioning? Handcuff me? Even pull out my fingernails? Actually all he did was give me a charming smile as he handed back my passport and say: 'You've been covering our referendum, haven't you, Mr Walker? You'll always be welcome.'

Either he was a secret member of the opposition or the news had not reached him that in the capital the Special Branch wanted to pull me in for questioning. A short walk to the Togolese border post, with huge Atlantic rollers crashing on the sands a few yards away, and I was safely out of Ghana.

My offence was that I had been reporting incidents which the military government did not want reported, and since I worked for the BBC World Service had been widely heard in

Ghana itself. The military leader in those days (1978) was a General Acheampong who had been in power for six years as the result of a coup. He wanted to legitimise his continued rule by introducing a bizarre political structure called union government under which the army (and police) would hold power together with some civilians. Wishing to put a democratic gloss on this proposal, he announced that there would be a nationwide referendum on it – then did his best to ensure that any opposition would remain unheard.

There was little interest in the referendum on the part of the Western press, but the BBC is listened to all over Africa, so as a London-based correspondent for the World Service I was sent to cover it. I soon discovered that there was a considerable and well-organised opposition denied access to the media. I also reported some of the dirty tricks the government was up to. For example, the judge who was supervising the referendum was threatened with death if he did not produce the result the government wanted. Then as the votes began to be counted a group of soldiers marched to his office demanding to be let in. Not surprisingly he took fright and fled, first to the home of a priest nearby, then to a safe house in the country.

The priest and a representative of the judge came to my hotel separately the next morning to tell me this extraordinary story, so far unreported. Their visits were conspiratorial. I had to be driven to a secret address in the country to hear the judge's version. The priest insisted on talking to me in the hotel gents, which must have given an odd impression to anyone watching from the lobby.

When I tried to put the story over on telex my copy was confiscated (for checking, the operator said), so I had to devise other means of getting it out. Telephone calls had to be booked at least a week in advance, but an audio-cassette and a helpful airline employee who carried it to London enabled the story to be broadcast the next day.

The local media had still not mentioned the incident, so the broadcast created something of a sensation in Ghana. So did my mention of claims that the vote was rigged (it was, of course). The next I heard – on Ghana Radio – was that investigations had shown that the soldiers were looking for a BBC reporter who had been sending false reports. Then I received a private warning that the Special Branch was looking for me and that it would be as well to make myself scarce. 'They might pull a few fingernails out before expelling you,' my informant said pleasantly. (Actually, this is a calumny; Ghanaians are among the most civilised and charming people in Africa.)

There were some interesting repercussions. Two British businessmen, one an MP, wrote separately and at a very high level to the BBC complaining about its coverage and the injustice done to 'that honest man' General Acheampong, with whom they had financial dealings. More relevant were letters to me from ordinary Ghanaians, grateful that some of the facts about their country's plight had been made public.

Some months later General Acheampong was forced to resign by his fellow-officers in the government. In the following year, after another military coup, he was executed by firing squad for crimes against the people. Cause and effect? Not directly, of course. But my reports were almost certainly a factor in the events that led to his downfall. They diminished his prestige and heartened the opposition. They contributed to the feeling that the regime of this 'honest man' was corrupt, inefficient and authoritarian, and in the end he had to go.

This story, not particularly important in itself, is nevertheless a good illustration of the way in which the BBC can affect the situation it is reporting. It is not in the business of toppling governments (and I certainly had no intention of doing so, just of reporting the facts). But for a short time it was the only source of news about important events in Ghana for the Ghanaians themselves as well as the rest of the world.

Nor is this episode unique. The BBC has been accused of undermining other governments — in Iran under the Shah, for example, in South Vietnam and in rather different circumstances and most dramatically in Liberia in 1990. The common factor is that it reported facts which the governments themselves tried to suppress and it was believed. It is difficult for people living in Western countries to understand the importance of international broadcasting in so many parts of the world. In the West there are many outlets for information. Even if governments try to influence television and to a lesser extent radio to say what they want, there are alternative pressures and alternative points of view available.

Even in Britain, where secretiveness is part of the culture, there is no need to listen to a foreign radio station to find out what is happening in your own country. But there are still countries where only information approved by the state is available. Even where this is not the case the media in Third World countries are usually under-developed by Western standards. Television, where it exists, still tends to be for the urban elite, newspapers are scrappy. Radio is the mass medium in these countries, but governments trying to ensure their own people are fed are unable to give it priority in development. This means there is an information gap to be filled. Broadcasters from many countries are anxious to fill it, crowding the short wave bands with their own version of the news and their attitude to it. International broadcasting is now undertaken by over 80 countries, from Afghanistan to Yugoslavia. They see it as a branch of diplomacy, a way of winning friends and influencing people or keeping in touch with their citizens abroad.

In this welter of words the BBC has a special position. It has been going for longer than most and gained a golden reputation during the war. The World Service has evolved as part of the BBC as a whole and not as a branch of government (unlike, for example the Voice of America) so it does not hesitate to report the views of those opposed to the government line whether at home or abroad. This is deliberate policy; in deed it is now so instinctive that it can hardly be described as policy at all. As we shall see it stems from the earliest days.

The British people, who pay for the World Service, are becoming increasingly aware of its existence but mostly unaware of the influence it wields. This is a pity. After all, it cost taxpayers £159 million (operating and capital budgets for broadcasting and monitoring) in the financial year 1991/92. For this they got an organisation which is fourth in the world in the number of hours broadcast ; it used to be fifth, but the addition of another language in October 1991 put it ahead of Germany, with over 800 hours a week. It claims the highest number of regular listeners – 120 million.

The World Service has been described (by an American journalist) as for the free mind what Oxfam is for the hungry and by others in rather less complimentary terms –' the mouthpiece of imperialism', for example. It is in fact peculiarly British in the haphazard way in which it developed, and its character derives ultimately from decisions made as long ago as the 1920s when 'wireless' was in its infancy....

The man who began it all. Guglielmo Marconi (1874 - 1937), right, presents a radiogram to Mr H. W. Allen at Marconi House in 1930.

CHAPTER ONE

Laying the Foundations

IN MARCH 1919, only a few months after the end of the First World War, the voice of a British wireless operator was heard nearly three thousand miles away across the Atlantic in the United States. This was probably the first external broadcast ever made from the British Isles – the transmitter was in Bally-bunion in Ireland – and was looked on at the time as uncanny.

However, it was in the nature of an experiment, and it was to be a number of years before such broadcasting came to be accepted as normal. Indeed, wireless telephony in its early days was regarded not so much as a way of relaying speech and music to millions of people simultaneously as an interesting new technique for sending messages between two points, like telegraphy.

At the beginning of the 20th century the Italian scientist Guglielmo Marconi, who had come to Britain, demonstrated that signals could be sent across the Atlantic by means of electro-magnetic waves without intervening wires. At first this was simply through a series of impulses – dots and dashes – although as early as 1906 the sound of a human voice was transmitted over a distance of several hundred miles in the United States.

Technical developments were stimulated by the First World War. Wireless was used for strictly military purposes during the war, but thousands of men were trained in its mysteries. Back in civilian life they became enthusiastic amateurs, building their own sets and listening in to the Morse code messages which filled the airwaves.

In order to operate their equipment they needed a licence. The Post Office had held a monopoly of telegram traffic for many years, so it undertook the task of issuing licences. In this way the Post Office became the government department most closely involved in the development of broadcasting. After the war it allowed manufacturers of radio equipment to carry out some experiments. The Ballybunion transmitter, for example, was set up by the Marconi company, the leader in the field. Marconi also transmitted some broadcasts from its headquarters at Chelmsford in Essex. They included speech and music – an amateur violinist, a pianist, singers. Some of these broadcasts were heard as far away as Madrid and Rome.

In 1920 the *Daily Mail* organised a half-hour transmission from Chelmsford by the Australian singer, Dame Nellie Melba.

Her voice was heard all over Europe and as far away as Newfoundland. As befitted the international flavour of the occasion, she sang in English, French and Italian, ending with a rendering of God Save the King. It was a great triumph.

The government then proceeded to ban any more experiments. This was because of objections by the military authorities who complained of interference with important messages. For example, an aircraft crossing the Channel in thick fog tried to obtain a weather report and could hear nothing but a woman singing.

However, other countries were developing wireless as a broadcasting medium. A series of regular concerts was being relayed from The Hague, and in the United States there was a great radio boom. It was the United States, in fact, which provided both an example and a warning to Britain and led indirectly to the creation of the BBC. Regular broadcasting began as early as 1916 in Philadelphia and led to large sales of receiving sets which in turn led to an extension of programmes. Other cities followed the example of Philadelphia, so that by May 1922 there were no fewer than 219 radio stations in the country transmit-ting regular programmes of news, talks and music, By the end of 1924 there were 530.

In Britain the natives were becoming rest-less. Radio amateurs wanted voices to listen to, manufacturers of sets wanted a home market. Even the military could not keep Britain behind the rest of the world for ever, and in 1922 the Post Office authorised the Marconi company to resume broadcasts. They came this time not from headquarters at Chelmsford but from a hut at Writtle, a few miles away, and they achieved a certain fame. The young men who organised them were engineers intent on exploring the technical possibilities of radio. But, faced with a microphone, they became performers and caught the imagination of their listeners

with their liveliness and informality.

A few months later the company was formed and 2LO was born. It was more serious than Writtle but just as pioneering. Transmissions, limited to one hour a day, went from a cinema at the top of Marconi House, in the Strand. Performers sometimes tripped over the wires leading to the microphone or passed comments on their work, not realising they were still on the air.

Companies other than Marconi were interested in opening stations – Metropolitan-Vickers in Manchester, for example, Western

Lord Reith (1889-1971), general manager and then Director General of the BBC from 1922 to 1938. Under his direction, shortwave broad-casting to the British Empire was inaugurated on 19 December, 1932.

Electric in Birmingham. But the Post Office was concerned that the problems in America, where stations interfered with each other and produced 'a jumble of signals' might be even worse in a smaller and more densely populated Britain. The Postmaster General told the House of Commons in April 1922: 'It would be impossible to have a large number of firms broadcasting. It would result only in a sort of chaos, only in a much more aggravated form than that which arises in the United States.'

The Post Office's preferred solution was to persuade the manufacturers to co-operate with each other in producing a broadcasting service. This was not originally seen as necessarily being a monopoly; one suggestion was that there might be two competing networks, each run by a number of individual companies. However, the Marconi company, which held a number of patents essential to

transmitter operations, said these would not be made available to any group of which Marconi was not a member.

So a monopoly it became, and the British Broadcasting Company was set up in October 1922 at a meeting attended by representatives of more than 200 firms. Revenue was to be raised from a fee which the Post Office would levy on receiving sets – the origin of the licence fee – and a royalty from each set sold. The company's object was to acquire a licence to create and operate radio stations to provide 'news, information, concerts, lectures, educational matters, speeches, weather reports, theatrical entertainment and any other matter which for the time being may be permitted...' The company advertised for a general manager at a salary of £1,750 a year. The successful candidate was John Reith, the son of a minister in the Free Church of Scotland. Reith created the BBC in his own

The hut at Writtle, in Essex, where Marconi engineers created the broadcasting station 2MT, in 1922.

image and elements of his philosophy remain, especially perhaps in the World Service.

Nowadays, particularly since his diaries were published, John Reith is generally thought to have been a forbidding, increasingly embittered man whose judgements were often clouded by personal obsessions. However, it is undeniable that he was also one of the few men of the time who saw the enormous possibilities of radio. He was convinced that these could be realised only if it were to be run as a public service, free of both governmental and commercial pressures. There was no money to be made from providing programmes, only from selling sets, so he met little opposition from the manufacturers who formed the board of the company. Accordingly, after a government enquiry, the company was wound up and the British Broadcasting Corporation formed under royal charter.

Instead of directors, the Corporation has a board of governors appointed by the government. This, of course, has its dangers. From time to time administrations of both political persuasions have appointed chairmen of the governors who are expected to 'sort out' the BBC, in other words make it more amenable to government influence. This aim has generally been frustrated because the new chairmen, whatever their attitudes before, tend to go native and support the BBC against the government. In fact, the charter and the licence and agreement which flow from it give the government considerable reserve powers – it can veto any programme, for example – but they have never been used.

The early BBC was admired both at home and abroad. It seemed to embody the best of all possible worlds and was held up as an example to less fortunate foreigners. A more sceptical age developed doubts. Here, for instance, is a broadside from the historian A.J.P. Taylor: 'Broadcasting became a dictatorship, as though Milton and others had never made the case for unlicensed utterance... Like all cultural dictatorships the BBC was more important for what it silenced than for what it achieved. Controllers ranked higher than producers in its hierarchy. Disturbing views were rarely aired. The English people, if judged by the BBC, were uniformly devout and kept always to the middle of the road.' (*English History, 1914-1945*, OUP 1963)

And the sociologist, Tom Burns, put it another way: 'The alternative view to that of the creation of the BBC as a shining example of British pragmatism...is that it was the most convenient and acceptable device for promoting radio broadcasting without burdening the government with the responsibility for the composition of programmes, or commercial undertakings with the cost of maintaining a service without benefit of advertising.' (*The BBC: Public Institution and Private World*, Macmillan 1977)

These revisionist criticisms were made well after the event when public opinion itself had changed. They were written after the BBC had lost its monopoly and adapted to competition, and television financed by advertising had shown it was not such a monster as its opponents once feared. The examples of 'unlicensed utterance' on television screens in other countries are not perhaps the sort of thing that Milton had in mind (striptease contests and game shows?), and the danger now seems one of declining standards and the BBC becoming marginalised.

A TV producer who has worked for both channels argued in 1988: 'I don't suppose that if broadcasting were invented to-day, we'd invent anything like the BBC, any more than we would re-invent the Royal Family. But both are there and work rather well and it seems a pity to lose either of them' (Antony Rouse, *The Times*, 17 February 1988). Reith would have enjoyed the comparison with the Royal Family. His own argument, as set down in 1950, was simple:

'It was the brute force of monopoly that enabled the BBC to become what it did; that made possible a policy in which moral responsibility – moral in the broadest way, intellectual and ethical – ranked high. If there is to be competition it will be of cheapness, not goodness.'

He refused to countenance the argument that radio should be used solely toprovide entertainment, giving people what they wanted: 'It is occasionally indicated tous that we are setting out to give the public what we think they need – and not what they want – but very few people know what they want and very few what they need...In any case it is better to over-estimate the mentality of the public than to underestimate it.'

This is rank heresy to-day, of course, and there is certainly something distasteful about the idea that the sombre vision of one man should be imposed on the nation. It is hardly surprising that arrogance and complacency are words which have come easily to critics of the BBC. But Reith's philosophy has not entirely disappeared; constraints were built into independent television when it was created in the fifties because of the standards already set by the BBC. And there is nothing inherently ignoble about seeking to use radio to enrich peoples' minds instead of to make

money out of them or subject them to political indoctrination.

The BBC under Reith assumed that Britain was a Christian country and must be encouraged to remain one. Staff had to comply with strict standards – divorce involved dismissal, for instance. Atheists and agnostics were unable to express their views on the air; even as late as the nineteen-fifties there was a tremendous row when a humanist was allowed to broadcast a talk expounding her disbelief in God. Programmes on Sundays consisted of church services, solemn music and solemn talks. Not surprisingly, competition developed in the form of commercially sponsored programmes directed at Britain from stations in Europe.

These stations drew their largest audiences in the morning, before the BBC came on the air with the daily religious service, and on Sundays. The programmes they offered were undemanding but fun – the *Ovalteenies*, for example; Sunny Jim, who advertised *Force* breakfast cereal, and a jingle for a meat extract which had the magnificent opening line: 'Hurrah for *Betox*, what a delightful smell!' Later one of the commercial stations – Radio Luxembourg – was to be used for altogether more serious purposes.

The BBC did not carry advertising; this

Published by The General Council of the Trades Union Congress

No. 4.   SATURDAY EVENING, MAY 8, 1926.   PRICE ONE PENNY

PEACE CALL SILENCED

Plan of Churches Not Broadcast

IS IT FAIR?

The Churches, under a sense of moral responsibility, have offered some leadership in this national

MISLEADING THE NATION

Our Reply to Sir John Simon's Innuendos and Charges

In his speech in the House of Commons on Thursday Sir John

SILENT ARSENAL AT WOOLWICH

"Not One Case of Blacklegging Reported"

50,000 OUT

From Our Special Correspondent
The silent strike holds sway in Woolwich. The great Arsenal and

A May 1926 issue of the TUC's strike bulletin, under the heading 'Peace call silenced', suggests partiality by the BBC. 'The churches… have put forward their view as to the basis of a possible concordat, but their voice has been officially silenced by the BBC, which is thus shown once more to be the instrument of the government.'

'This programme is being radiated by the Empire Transmitters'

Do you hear the Empire Programmes? Daily, the Empire Transmissions broadcast a programme that caters for every taste—symphony and promenade concerts, talks, dance music, vaudeville. These programmes provide a live link with the Motherland! A link that enables those who are situated in the far flung corners of the world to enjoy the wealth of entertainment the Motherland offers. Those who miss the programmes of the Empire Transmitter are missing the finest broadcasts that the world has ever known.

Eelex Short Wave Convertors utilise ALL THE VALVES of your present set, thus the power of your set is increased, and you can receive England, Europe and the World!

No alteration is necessary to your present set.

Testimonials show that as many as 100 extra stations have been logged by satisfied users.

Can you receive England, Europe and the World?

— Fit an Eelex Short-Wave Convertor to your present set and you will!

DUPLEX CONVERTOR.	B2 CONVERTOR.	M2 SUPER CONVERTOR (as illustrated)
Single valve instrument for Battery, A.C. or D.C. mains receivers. Covers 15-60 Metres.	Two valve instrument for battery operation. Covers 15-60 Metres.	Two valve instrument A.C. Mains operated. Powerful results on 15-60 Metres.
58/- (Battery)	£4 : 18 : 0 complete.	£8 : 15 : 0 complete.
66/- (Mains) complete.		Extra coil suitable for each type of convertor available, covering 60-120 Metres approx. 2 6 each

Write for booklet No. O.M.S. giving further particulars.

J. J. EASTICK & SONS,
EELEX HOUSE,
118, BUNHILL ROW, LONDON, E.C.1.
Telegrams : MET. 0314 5 6.

Advertising hyperbole from 'The Daily Mirror Overseas Edition' of December, 1934. Adding this gadget to the wireless set would allow listeners overseas to enjoy 'the wealth of entertainment the Motherland offers. Those who miss the programmes of the Empire Transmitter are missing the finest broadcasts that the world has ever known.'

was ruled out from the beginning although Reith did once suggest it as a supplementary source of income to the licence fee. The chief reason was pressure from newspaper owners. They were afraid of losing money to this upstart new medium and behaved in the usual way of powerful interests threatened by technical advance – try to minimise its impact. For the same reason they hampered the BBC in developing its news service. It was not allowed at first to prepare its own bulletins; they were provided by the news agencies who were given credit for them on the air. They could not be broadcast before 7 pm, so as not to damage the sales of evening papers. Although some of these restrictions were eased later, it was not until the outbreak of war in 1939 that the BBC was able to carry news in its domestic services before 6 pm. Now, of course, it never seems to stop.

The general strike of 1926 provided a temporary exception to these rules and forced the BBC to set up its own news section. All the national newspapers disappeared from the streets and radio bulletins at various times of the day were a vital source of information. But the BBC came under enormous pressure, to some of which it succumbed.

A section of the Cabinet, led by Winston Churchill, wanted to take the organisation over and use it as a government mouthpiece similar to the British Gazette which Churchill edited free of any concern with such tedious concepts as objectivity. The majority of the Cabinet disagreed. Reith, aware of the threat in the background, took a very circumspect line.

He accepted the 'advice' of the government to deny air time to the Labour Party leader, Ramsay Macdonald, and the Archbishop of Canterbury, who wanted to make an appeal for moderation which conflicted at points

King George V broadcasts his 1934 Christmas message to home and Empire from Sandringham.

with government policy. Mistakes were made in the news bulletins and in some places the BBC became known as the BFC – the British Falsehood Company. On the other hand the bulletins did contain statements from the strike leaders, not just those from the government. And Reith confided to his diary that when he met Churchill, 'I told him that if we put out nothing but government propaganda we should not be doing half the good that we were' – an early example of a theme that is to recur. In fact, Reith felt that the government had placed the organisation in a difficult position by neither taking it over nor allowing it complete freedom.

More than half a century later a chairman of the BBC governors, Sir Michael Swann (as he was then) argued that the tradition of impartiality which the BBC built up began in the period after the strike in which its weakness had been exposed. He said: 'It seems to have been something of a fortunate accident in that the government of the day did not realise the full political potential of broadcasting while the press of the day were very jealous of the infant BBC, with the result that political news and comment were very much restricted and the political problem only slowly emerged. Reith, however, understood the problem and from an early stage set about creating the tradition of impartiality. There still exists his scribbled comment on a minute asking for advice on how to handle some problem and it reads: 'Give both sides. As a result, as the restrictions were lifted, the BBC acquired sufficient credit for impartiality not to alarm the politicians unduly.' (From a lecture at the University of Salford, 1978)

The qualities which Reith fostered in the BBC – cultural and moral uplift, political impartiality combined with deference to authority – were to be applied not only to broadcasting in Britain but also to that directed overseas.

From the very beginning of radio, Reith saw that it had international ramifications. For one thing, wavelengths had to be allocated by negotiation between various countries so as to avoid undue interference and this alone took several years. But the new technology might also be used to bring the countries of the Empire closer together. As Reith put it in 1925: 'All our colonial concerns are now looking to us to suggest something from which they will benefit.' One way was to send them BBC men to help them set up their own broadcasting systems. But direct broadcasting from London was another matter; there were technical and financial problems to overcome.

Transmissions to the home audience were carried on long or medium waves which, depending on various factors, could be heard several hundred miles away. For long-distance broadcasting it was necessary to use short waves which are reflected from the ionosphere – a layer of electrically charged gases miles above the earth. They are then reflected back to the ionosphere from the earth and so on, reaching their destination in a series of 'hops'.

The Americans began short-wave broadcasting in 1924 and the Russians in 1925, but the BBC took rather longer. Their chief engineer explained loftily in 1927: 'We stayed our hand so as not to put out noises combined with all sorts of atmospherics and inaccuracies and periods of silence and general unpleasantness, merely to satisfy what might be called the sentimental feeling abroad just to hear something which is neither music nor intelligent speech.'

Sentimental they may have been, but if people living in the Empire could hear Philadelphia why should they not expect to hear London? Many of them did and complained at the lack. Britain seemed to be lagging behind again in making the best use of the new medium. The government, which was keen to see some sort of service directed at the Empire, encouraged the BBC to start experimental short wave broadcasting from the Marconi works in Chelmsford in 1927.

Government encouragement, however, was only verbal and the vital question of finance for the new service was left unresolved. Reith argued that the money received from licence fees was intended to improve the service to British listeners only – after all, it was their money. The Dominions, which had just had their complete independence recognised, refused to contribute anything; they were more interested in building up their own broadcasting services. The Colonial Office, although enthusiastic, said it could not bear the whole cost. The curious feature of the affair, seen from sixty years on, is the small amount of money involved in a wrangle which went on for several years.

In 1930 the BBC estimated that it would cost £40,000 to build a transmitting station at Daventry which would need to be replaced after five years. It would cost £7,000 a year to maintain and, with 1,700 hours of broadcasting a year, programmes would take another £34,000; an alternative scheme cut this to £22,000. The BBC pointed out: 'No new body, whether of public service or commercial constitution, would be able to provide the service at lower cost, since such a body would not have the benefit of British Broadcasting Corporation general programme expenditure, not to mention its experience and organisation.'

Oddly enough the financial problem was settled by the economic crisis of 1931, which led to the formation of a national government. Cuts in government spending were announced, and as part of its contribution to the nation's finances the BBC agreed to carry the cost of Empire broadcasting. It made an implicit apology for using licence

From the earliest days of broadcasting, music was an important part of the output. The chimes in the background of this studio were used to give the time signal

fees in this way: 'The British listener's direct interest in this project is of course, nil, but the question of national interests had to be looked at more broadly.'

The Daventry transmitter was built, able to operate on eight short wave bands, and broadcasting to the Empire – precursor of to-day's World Service – began on 19 December 1932. It was inaugurated formally by the Chairman of the BBC governors, J.H. Whitley, followed by Reith, who spoke of radio as becoming 'a connecting and co-ordinating link between the scattered parts of the British Empire.' The service, he said, would be dedicated to the best interests of mankind.

There were five separate transmissions a day, of two hours each, directed so as to reach listeners in the peak listening hours of the evening in different parts of the world. Reith had to read his message at the beginning of each transmission at intervals during the day, into the small hours of the morning 'I was very bored with it and with having to speak for about twelve minutes,' he noted in his diary.

Six days later came the great occasion, the first royal broadcast to the Empire. King George V delivered a Christmas message to his subjects, beginning a tradition that has lasted to this day:

'Through one of the marvels of modern science, I am enabled this Christmas day to speak to all my peoples throughout the Empire…I speak now from my home and from my heart to you all, to men and women so cut off by the snows and the deserts or the seas that only voices out of the air can reach them. To those cut off from fuller life by blindness, sickness or infirmity, and to those who are celebrating this day with their children and grandchildren, to all, to each, I wish a happy Christmas. God bless you.'

Among those celebrating with the king were, of course, his own children and grandchildren, among whom was the future Queen Elizabeth II, then six years old.

Broadcasting to the Empire had its own particular problems in engineering and programming. The technical side was explained by the BBC as follows: 'Consider the case of a transmission from England to New Zealand. The time in England being 8 am GMT and the date June 1st. It will be summer in England and daylight; over mid-Russia the sun time (the term sun time is used to differentiate from the mean or clock time of the district) will be three hours later, ie, 11am; over Mongolia (Lake Baikal) the sun time will be seven hours later, viz, 1500 or 3 pm; over New Guinea in the equatorial region the time will be nine hours later, viz, 1700; over Brisbane, ten hours later – 1800 or 6 pm midwinter, when it will be dark; in New Zealand the sun time will be 1940 or 7.40, midwinter and again dark. In this case it will be necessary to choose a wave which will be efficiently transmitted by the Heaviside Layer (ionosphere) when the greater part of the path is in daylight and summer conditions, but some of it in darkness and winter conditions.'

Most programmes were taken from the output of the domestic services, then divided into National and Regional outlets. They included light music, variety and commentaries relayed live on such events as test matches, Wimbledon and the boat race. But some items were produced especially for the Empire Service – a commemoration of Anzac Day, for instance, beamed to the Australasian zone, talks, a concert by 'representative overseas artists.' The service acquired its own news section in 1934.

Because of its varied transmission times the Empire Service had to rely to some extent on recorded or, as they were known at first, 'bottled' programmes. A concert originally broadcast during the early evening, for example, would be recorded for use in the late night transmission. The techniques were fairly primitive compared to what is available now. They involved cutting a wax disc, which gave a playing time of between five and nine minutes, or using what was called the Blattner system. This made a magnetic record on a fine steel tape which was rolled up on a drum like a cinema film. In this way it was possible to make a recording lasting up to 20 minutes. However, the tape was too expensive to enable such a recording to be stored; it was often transferred to disc, the tape wiped clean and used again.

The system had its faults, as Robert Dougall, who began his announcing career in the Empire Service, recalled: 'Apart from changes in pitch known as "Wow" and a mysterious interference called "Plop" , the main trouble with the beastly Blattner was that the tape all too often broke. The engineer would then go quietly mad, trying to stick the two ends together again, while the announcer apologised and played fill-up records.

'There was another diabolical trick the Blattnerphone could play. It did it to me once when, with a flourish of trumpets I had announced a speech by His Royal Highness the Duke of Gloucester, and thereupon ensued a noise like the high-pitched chattering of monkeys at the zoo. To my horror I realised the tape was being played backwards. At least I learned to be a good apologiser, which served me well later, when television came along.' (*In and Out of the Box*, Collins and Harvill Press, 1973))

Several changes were made in the first few years of the service. New transmitters were built at Daventry and the hours of broadcasting increased, until shortly before the outbreak of war in 1939 the service was on the air for 18 hours day. A BBC Empire Orchestra was created. Relays of such national events with international appeal as the Silver Jubilee of George V in 1935 and the abdication broadcast of Edward VIII in 1936 were heard in many parts of the world.

But the formal and staid approach of the BBC was not universally popular. The corporation's representative in New York – where radio was very different – argued that Empire Service programmes were 'flabby and uninspired and had no real relation whatever with the needs and tastes of listeners in different lands.' There were reports of English listeners in India turning off their sets because they found nothing worth listening to. The BBC might have a monop-oly in Britain, but it did not have one in the world.

There were several countries which took short-wave broadcasting more seriously than Britain did. They were prepared to invest heavily in it, not just money but ideas as well. One example of this, as the BBC explained plaintively in 1936, was the difficulty it experienced in trying to persuade artists to broadcast for the Empire Service at times when most people were in bed: 'In certain other countries (Germany and Italy, for instance) the relation of the state authority to artists is such as to make their services more easily available at these awkward hours than is possible in Great Britain.'

Germany and Italy, of course, were dictator-ships. During the thirties they were develop-ing new, strident forms of broadcasting which were winning listeners.

Before long the BBC was to stop making excuses and face the challenge.

CHAPTER TWO

The Totalitarian Challenge

IN THE UNITED STATES, radio became a branch of salesmanship, in Britain a public service monopoly, insulated as far as possible from party politics. But there were countries in which it was seen as a marvellous new political asset, to be used solely to spread the point of view of the government or the ruling party. This is still the position in much of the world to-day, particularly in the newer medium of television. How many news bulletins in developing countries open with obligatory shots of the country's leader, making a speech, laying a foundation stone, getting into or out of an aircraft, in general creating an image of ubiquity and power?

The Germans and the Russians were pioneers in using radio as a political weapon. The Germans began as early as 1915 by putting out a regular Morse code service of news as seen from Berlin to the neutral countries with which their cable links had been cut. They also used the service to carry coded messages to their agents.

On the day the Russian revolution began, 7 November 1917, a message to the citizens of Russia, drafted by Lenin, was transmitted from the cruiser *Aurora* lying at St. Petersburg. It was followed by other transmissions, including one on 12 November announcing the formation of a Soviet government.

Before long, messages were being directed abroad to explain the purposes of the revolution. On 4 February 1918 Lenin issued a radio report 'to every-one' designed to counteract what were described as false reports in foreign newspapers. Later came broadcasts directed to particular countries. In 1919, for instance, workers in Britain, France and Italy were asked to demonstrate against intervention in the Soviet Union.

The first broadcast in a foreign language – German – came in 1920, but it was not until nine years later that foreign language transmissions were organised on a regular basis, beginning with German, French and English. By 1933, when the BBC Empire Service in English had just begun, the Soviet Union was broadcasting regularly in eight languages.

Soviet propaganda, although given to jargon, was not without effect. As early as 1932 the Foreign Office was expressing concern about its penetration into Palestine and the Persian Gulf, areas in which Britain had substantial interests. But it was innocuous by comparison with what was to follow from Nazi Germany and Fascist Italy.

Hitler believed that propaganda had played a decisive part in the allied victory in the First World War, thus by implication excusing the defeat of the German army. He likened it to an artillery bombardment before an infantry attack and devoted considerable thought to the subject. In a modern analysis of Hitlerism, the German historian Joachim Fest wrote: 'Propaganda was the genius of National Socialism. Not only did it owe to propaganda its most important successes; propaganda was its one and only original contribution to the conditions for its rise and was always more than an instrument of power; propaganda was part of its essence.' (*The Face of the Third Reich,* by Joachim C. Fest, English translation Weidenfeld and Nicolson, 1970)

Nazi propaganda was flexible, varying its approach according to the objective. It could use truth, half truths, lies, abuse and threats; the only criterion was whether or not it succeeded in its aim. It was well suited to the new medium of radio which Hitler used to relay his speeches with their violent rhetoric. Radio propaganda played a part in securing a vote in the Saarland in favour of a return to Germany; it projected an image of German might which terrorised ordinary people in Europe. One consequence was that governments in other countries, including Britain, accepted Hitler's estimation and attached more importance to propaganda than it warranted – and the word itself became debased from its original meaning which was simply 'to propagate the faith'.

When they came to power in 1933 the Nazis took over a short wave station at Zeesen, a village about 20 miles south-east of Berlin. Transmissions were directed at first in English and German to North America. This was where the largest number of people of German origin lived outside the Third Reich itself, and the early broadcasts were intended to rally Germans overseas to the Nazi cause, including its anti-semitism.

In the following years the number of languages increased; they came eventually to include such unlikely tongues as Gaelic and

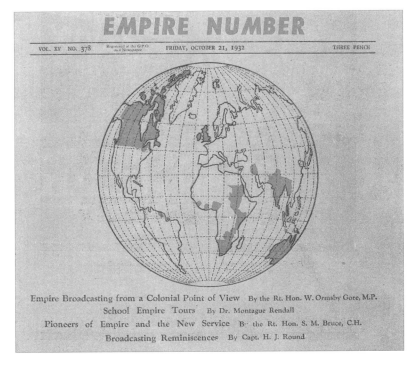

An October 1932 issue of World Radio. *The shaded areas on the globe show, with only slight exaggeration, the British Empire.*

Dr Joseph Goebbels, Minister of Public Enlightenment and Propaganda, broadcasting Hitler's proclamation on Austria from Berlin in March, 1938.

Afrikaans, the former directed to disaffected Scots, the latter to actual or potential sympathisers in South Africa. Zeesen developed practices which are still used to-day by other broadcasters, including the BBC. Among them were the encouragement of letters from listeners, some read over the air, the organisation of competitions and the free distribution of programme details. It organised listening groups and went to great lengths to suit programmes to particular countries. This was done by such devices as celebrating national days and tailoring comments to the audience. For instance, the service in Hindustani to India, then under British rule, once said: 'We, the German people, respect Mahatma Gandhi just as much as we respect Hitler, who has the same principles as Gandhi. National Socialism, too, teaches non-violence.' Whether or not any Indian listeners believed this improbable statement is not recorded.

A more belligerent tone was adopted in broadcasts to the Soviet Union: 'Clippings from Soviet newspapers exposing the less savoury aspects of conditions in the Union are read and commented upon. Particular

attention is called to the names of Jewish or supposedly Jewish officials in Russia. After every name the speakers emit a loud, raucous and somewhat melodramatic "Ha! Ha!"'. (*The Political Use of the Radio* by Thomas Grandin, Geneva Research Centre, 1939)

Broadcasting to the Arab world was at first undertaken on behalf of the Axis by the Fascist government in Italy. In support of their invasion of Abyssinia (Ethiopia) in 1935 the Italians used a radio station in Bari, southern Italy, to carry on a bitter campaign against British 'imperialism'. It was directed in particular towards countries where there was a strong British presence, such as Palestine and Egypt. Palestine was a particularly promising target. Britain administered it as a League of Nations mandate with a pledge to provide a national home for Jews there. After Hitler came to power in Germany Jewish immigration became a torrent of people fleeing persecution. This in turn produced a violent reaction from the indigenous Arabs who began a military revolt against the British.

The Italian broadcasts were a mixture of entertainment and propaganda, including accounts of alleged British atrocities and such edifying comments as 'The Empire of the British is decadent', 'The British fleet is a museum piece' and 'Eden (the Foreign Secretary) is a clown in the hands of the Freemasons.' Radio sets locked to Italian stations were reported to be distributed free or at very low cost to cafes and other places where Arabs congregated in large numbers.

When Britain recognised the Italian conquest of Abyssinia, a 'gentlemen's agreement' was reached between the two governments. The Italians agreed to stop hostile broadcasts. At moments of tension they were revived, but the main target of Bari became the French territories in North Africa. But this did not mean any respite for the British. From 1938 the Nazis began broadcasting in Arabic. They did so in a thorough fashion, hiring Arab lecturers from German universities and Arab exiles from countries under British domination. Their material – again a seductive mixture of popular entertainment and atrocity stories – was often reproduced by local newspapers and radio stations. Even the king of Iraq sent out anti-British stories taken from the German radio on his own amateur station. When the British protested the Iraqi prime minister replied that he could not control the king.

In 1934 both the Italians and the Germans began broadcasting to Latin America, where many people from the two countries had settled. There were governments which could be influenced to follow a friendly policy, and there was the bonus of 'Yankee imperialism' to be attacked with popular support. Short-wave transmissions could reach only a limited number of people, so great emphasis was laid on local re-broadcasting. Not only was material provided free; the local stations were allowed to insert their own commercials, so making a profit. In some cases private stations were subsidised or bought outright.

The Italians were able to make great play with the Roman Catholic sympathies of much of the population. In their broadcasts to the Arabs they portrayed Mussolini as the defender of Islam. In Latin America he changed his faith and became the leader of the great Christian nation fighting atheistic Communism and Anglo-American plutocracy. The Italians had another good idea which has been taken up by later broadcasters. They introduced Italian lessons by radio in a variety of foreign languages. They read out Mussolini's speeches as texts for dictation. Listeners could send their work to Rome for correction, and when it got back programme details and Fascist propaganda leaflets were enclosed.

In the light of all this it is hardly surprising that the possibility of Britain taking part in the radio war had to be seriously considered – although nobody in those days would have admitted that it was a war. The Ullswater Committee, which in 1936 reported on the future of the BBC (and said its monopoly should continue) gave its blessing to the Empire Service and added: 'In the interest of British prestige and influence in world affairs we think the appropriate use of languages other than English should be encouraged. We trust that the effects of these recommendations will be to foster mutual understanding within the British Commonwealth of Nations and beyond it.' It was hardly a call to battle.

Other voices joined in. Mabel Strickland, owner of *The Times of Malta*, wrote to the *Sunday Times* of London complaining about the Italian broadcasts which could be heard clearly on her Mediterranean island. 'It is more than time this twisting of the lion's tail should cease,' she said. 'Forever turning the other cheek is misunderstood on the Mediterranean littoral and is taken as a sign of decadence, of which disease we are being hourly accused.'

The government and the BBC set up

separate committees to examine the possibilities of broadcasting in foreign languages. There was no certainty that it would be the job of the corporation. The government committee toyed with the idea of a medium wave station in Cyprus controlled by the Foreign Office. Behind this lay the thought that the BBC was dragging its feet over the issue and also that with its tiresome insistence on giving both sides, it might not be the ideal body to take on the hard-hitting, if inaccurate, Axis propaganda machine. As far as the BBC was concerned there was opposition on the part of those running the Empire Service on the grounds that broadcasting in foreign languages was bound to be seen as propaganda – a hate-word in the Corporation – and lessen the credibility of the existing service. One suggestion for overcoming this objection was that the Foreign Office should prepare the transmissions, using the technical facilities of the BBC which, whiter than white, would make it clear that it bore no responsibility for the contents.

Reith understood the objections of his executives, but he had believed for a number of years that the BBC should be speaking in tongues. The plans for a transmitter in Cyprus were shelved on technical grounds, and the Cabinet committee finally asked the BBC for its proposals. With the internal argument at an end, Reith set out the agreed position. Foreign language broadcasts, he said, should not prejudice the Empire Service; the BBC should undertake them if they were to be undertaken at all; they would have to be done on a considerable scale, including not merely news bulletins but sustaining programmes as well; special finance would be needed; and the BBC should have the same freedom vis-a-vis government departments as it had with its home service.

It would increase its contacts with the Foreign Office, but it must be responsible for the contents of the transmissions. Reith was talking about broadcasts in Arabic and in Spanish and Portuguese for Latin America. The head of the Foreign Office News Department, Rex Leeper, argued that there should be a distinction between the two sets of audiences, those in Latin America being 'sophisticated and Westernised'. He was in favour of what he called 'an innocent form of propaganda for the Arab world, that is, selecting news items which were in the interests of the country and omitting those which in the view of the Foreign Office it would be inadvisable should be given the emphasis that broadcasting by wireless would give.'

This argument, attractive to the official mind with its assumption that the Foreign Office always knows best, was to return in different guises, but the BBC never accepted it. Reith conceded that the corporation might be more amenable to Foreign Office views in the case of Arabic than other languages because of the delicate situation in the Middle East. But he reiterated the need for independence from government control and said prestige depended on broadcasting that was both truthful and comprehensive – in other words not leaving out items which might be embarrassing.

Matters were finally arranged more or less to his satisfaction. At the end of October 1937 the Postmaster-General said in the House of Commons that the BBC would undertake broadcasts in certain foreign languages and that it would deal in straight news, not propaganda. The announcement – in answer to a question – was presented as a purely governmental one, and Reith protested that it was of cardinal importance that it should be known that this was to be a BBC, not a government, service. A few days later the Chancellor of the Exchequer therefore made a further statement to the effect that the corporation had been invited by the government to broadcast in Spanish and Portugese to South America and to the Middle East in Arabic. Sir John Simon added that the BBC would have the same responsibilities and duties in respect of the new services as it had with its existing ones and the government was satisfied it would maintain the same high standards.

The government's real concern was with the Middle East and the Italian broadcasts in Arabic. But this was the age of appeasement, and, absurd as it may seem now, Mussolini was seen as a potential ally. To broadcast only in Arabic might look like a direct challenge; so Latin America, where Britain had commercial but not strategic interests, was added; it is unlikely that Mussolini was fooled.

Reith was happy with the wording of the second Parliamentary announcement, but the detailed arrangements were ambiguous and not entirely satisfactory. Eden, the Foreign Secretary of the day, thought there should be a written agreement between the

With such a headline, few newspapers were left unsold on that first Sunday in September, 1939.

Foreign Office and the BBC, but the British preference for fuzzy edges asserted itself and instead there was a 'gentleman's agreement' between Reith and Vansittart, the Permanent Under-Secretary, which the two parties tended to interpret differently.

On the financial side the government agreed to pay the BBC to run the new service on a year by year basis.

According to Reith's biographer, he would have done better to insist on a written guarantee of long-term financial support: 'Anthony Eden's demand for a written accord might have given rise to problems of interpretation. Yet an uncovenanted grant-in-aid, in strict accordance with the BBC's actual needs, was the greater of two evils. The corporation would from now on depend increasingly on the grace and favour of the Treasury and the Foreign Office, and the BBC as never before would be held to ransom when economic troubles loomed or when ministers and anonymous advisers took it into their heads to grind political axes at the slightest whim.' (*Only the Wind will Listen,* Andrew Boyle, Hutchinson, 1972)

Fair comment, as the number of cuts made or threatened for reasons of expediency show. But, of course, it is based on hindsight; nobody in 1937 could have foreseen the enormous growth in the service in the next few years. And, even if this had been possible, no government is likely to give a guarantee of unlimited funds for an indefinite future in order to pay for broadcasting.

The grant-in-aid continues to this day, since no better system seems to have been found. But it is now given on a rolling three year basis (with increases for inflation) to make advance planning easier.

The 'gentleman's agreement' led, as might have been expected, to a certain confusion. After a meeting with BBC representatives Rex Leeper wrote down what he thought had been agreed. He said the BBC should regard the foreign language services as

31

something quite apart from the Home and Empire Services because 'they are intended to have a direct effect on our relations with foreign countries.' He therefore thought it permissible to omit harmful items of news (economy with the truth, as it would be called to-day); if they had to be included there should be an explanatory comment.

The BBC attitude was quite other, as the very first Arabic news bulletin – on 3 January 1938 – was to show.

The third item was an embarrassing one which began: 'Another Arab of Palestine was executed by hanging at Acre this morning by order of a military court. He was arrested during recent riots in the Hebron mountains and was found to possess a rifle and ammunition.'

This story, harmless enough by to-day's standards, caused shock and dismay in the Arab world – and the Foreign Office. The King of Saudi Arabia is reported to have wept when he heard the news, and an Iraqi newspaper went into a paroxysm of rage: 'The London radio inaugurated its Arabic programmes by the broadcast of acts of terror in Palestine and of the execution of Arab Muslim youths (sic) – a proceeding which even the most Zionist of Zionists would pronounce as representing a lack of taste, to say the least.'

Rex Leeper seemed to think the gentleman's agreement had been violated. 'Is the BBC to broadcast to the Empire the execution of every Arab in Palestine?' he asked rhetorically. 'It seems to me unnecessary, though I suspect it gives their conscience a warm glow.'

The bulletin has since become part of BBC folklore, an example of how from the very beginning the foreign language services showed their independence. The ethos Reith had fostered in the BBC made it impossible for the story to be ignored. It had already been broadcast in the Empire Service and, if it had been omitted from a bulletin meant for the Arab world, the credibility of the new service would have been destroyed from the beginning.

Nevertheless, there were heartsearchings in the BBC as well as elsewhere. The Arabic sub-editor, A.S. Calvert, recruited from the consular service, asked for guidance from his

The BBC started overseas broadcasting services in Arabic in January, 1938. Visitors to the opening included the Governor of Aden and representatives from Saudi Arabia, Yemen, Iraq and Egypt.

superior, J.B. Clark, then in charge of the Empire Service. The reply was a clear, if slightly bureaucratic, expression of principle which *mutatis mutandis* still obtains to-day: 'There is no question about the object of the service: it is to serve the best interests of Great Britain and the Empire. But there may be different ways of achieving this object.. selection of news is of great importance and needs expert knowledge of an audience and background...but the omission of unwelcome facts of news and the consequent suppression of truth runs counter to the corporation's policy laid down by the appropriate authority.'

The storm over the first bulletin soon died down. A fortnightly series of liaison meetings was set up between the Foreign Office and the BBC. British embassies in Arab countries searched for items which might be included. The main problem became how to improve the service. In its first few weeks it was criticised in a report by a senior lecturer at the London School of Oriental Studies as being 'lifeless and dry' with little news of interest to Arabs.

The corporation recruited some British Arabists and a number of talented Arabs, including a poet and a man described as the best Arabic announcer in the world.

Arabic music became a regular feature, as did talks especially written for the service; there was even a commentary on the Grand National. By September the BBC was able to reply to critics who complained that its programmes were less exciting than those from Zeesen or Bari by comparing itself rather pompously to a quality newspaper 'of sober authenticity' rather than one which was concerned solely with circulation.

The Latin American service followed that in Arabic by only just over two months; the inaugural broadcast went out in the small hours of 15 March 1938. After the Empire Service closed down at 1.30 am there was a fifteen-minute transmission in Spanish,

followed by one in Portuguese for Brazil. The timing, of course, was dictated by the fact that South and Central America are several hours behind GMT, and the transmissions were aimed at the peak listening hours of the evening. It also enabled the service to open in style, with a champagne buffet supper in Broadcasting House attended by ambassadors from Latin American countries and other VIPs. To while away the time before transmission they listened to music played by an augmented BBC Empire orchestra – Elgar, Manuel de Falla, Villa Lobos and Milhaud. A message from the director-general was read over the air.

When new transmitters were completed, and it was possible to extend the service to three hours a night – July 1939 – there was another champagne supper. By then there was a new director-general – F.W. Ogilvie, formerly vice-chancellor of Queen's university, Belfast. He was able to read his own message in Spanish, although not in Portuguese. The music was different too – Joe Loss and his orchestra and Billy Mayerl on the piano.

Although the Latin American service was originally conceived as a kind of smokescreen for the Arabic service, it developed its own audience.

The BBC North American representative showed what it was up against in a report he submitted after touring the continent: 'We are facing damaging propag-anda in all its forms, propaganda concerted, skilful, highly organised and prosecuted with resourcefulness and infinite diligence. Day by day the prestige of Britain is belittled; our motives misconstrued or distorted; our smallest difficulties exaggerated.'

This sounds a little over-dramatic. In any case half an hour or even three hours of broadcasting a day was unlikely to be an effective riposte, particularly considering the size and diversity of the area; it comprised some sixteen separate states with varied

In Oxford Street, Poland dominates the war news in Selfridges windows in 1939. A board with the 'Latest War News' reports enemy aircraft off East Anglia. 'They did not penetrate our defences and no damage has been reported'. The more prudent window-shoppers are carrying their gas masks.

cultural, economic and geographical backgrounds. All the same the BBC was able to arrange re-broadcasts by a number of local stations despite charging a small fee.

Listening seems to have increased at the time of the Munich crisis of September 1938. A listener in Cuba, for example, sent 'sincere and cordial congratulations on the impartiality, sound judgement and common sense with which the London station has kept its innumerable Spanish speaking listeners informed of European events.'

The Munich crisis marked an important phase in the story of the World Service. It arose from Hitler's claim to parts of Czechoslovakia, and for a time war seemed imminent. At six o'clock in the evening of 27 September, in a sudden reversal of previous policy, the Foreign Office asked the BBC to transmit in French, German and Italian the text of a broadcast by the Prime Minister, Neville Chamberlain.

Cecilia Gillie, who later became a leading member of the French service (and married its wartime head Darsie Gillie) has described the chaotic situation which resulted: 'No

one in the BBC realised how long it took to make a translation of this kind. Finally a human chain was made from typing room to studios, and sheets passed from hand to hand...Walter Goetz, who made the broadcast in German, told me how he was telephoned by J.B. Clark, then Acting Controller (Overseas) at a cocktail party and asked to come to the BBC on urgent business – ignoring the traffic lights if necessary. He drove at all speed to Broadcasting House and, a little stunned as he had never broadcast before, and had in addition been drinking vodka, agreed to read the text which was given to him page by page.' (From an unpublished account of the *French Service Wartime Transmissions*, BBC archives)

The whole broadcast could not be translated in time, and he had to end at the famous passage about 'a quarrel in a far away country of which we know nothing', which must have left an unfortunate impression on any German who happened to hear it. These broadcasts were put out not only on the short wave frequencies of the Empire Service but also on the medium wavebands used by the domestic services. This not unnaturally led to protests from British listeners, some of whom actually went to Broadcasting House to make their feelings known. One man wrote in to complain that it was against public policy to allow the Germans and Italians to take over radio in the evening because 'they are both against the British.'

There is no evidence that the broadcasts were heard by those for whom they were intended, but the next day, according to W.J. West (*Truth Betrayed,* Duckworth 1987) a German translation of Chamberlain's broadcast was transmitted from Radio Luxembourg – which already had an audience in Germany.

In spite of this confused start the BBC continued to broadcast in French, German and Italian. In April 1939, after Hitler had marched into what was left of Czechoslovakia, they were established as three separate services and their hours increased. The Foreign Office at first contested Ogilvie's argument that they should be on the same basis as the existing foreign language services – that is, with the BBC, not the Foreign Office determining the contents. Lord Halifax, now Foreign Secretary, referred to the 'delicate relationship' with Germany and said: 'The BBC could hardly be expected to possess sufficient knowledge of the facts to enable it always to be the best judge of what should or should not be included in a bulletin.'

This was Rex Leeper's argument all over again. Its persistence suggests an unwilling admiration for Nazi propaganda, which used radio as a guided weapon not as a disinterested purveyor of facts, which is how the BBC saw its role. Halifax was eventually persuaded that the BBC should retain responsibility for the broadcasts, provided there were regular informal contacts with the Foreign Office.

As war came closer, services to foreign countries increased. An English service to Europe was inaugurated in November and May 1939 saw the beginning of a weekly newsletter in Afrikaans on the Empire Service. This was a direct response to broadcasts from Germany, but it does not seem to have set the veldt alight. It was simply a translation of what had already gone out in English. Things improved later, with increased hours and the addition of a news bulletin, but the BBC had to contend with a dearth of good Afrikaner speakers in Britain.

In June, broadcasts began in Spanish and Portuguese for Europe; at the end of August, after the Nazi-Soviet non-aggression pact, the hours of the German service were increased. On 30 August the service transmitted a message to the German people from the National Council of Labour.

The message had actually been published five days earlier; the government forbade the German service to carry it, then changed its mind. Ogilvie thought the service should broadcast the sound of the famous BBC nightingale as a token of Britain's peaceful intentions, but by that time it would have taken more than a nightingale to change the course of events.

The Nazis had been jamming BBC broadcasts experimentally for several months, and on the day Britain and France declared war – 3 September 1939 – listening to the BBC was made illegal in Germany.

These measures were a sign of one of the weaknesses of German propaganda; it could not tolerate alternative versions, however muffled.

This did not matter much as long as the Nazis were militarily successful, but once they began to suffer defeats even the threat of the death penalty could not keep Germans from listening to the BBC.

CHAPTER THREE

V for Victory

WHEN WAR broke out the BBC was already broadcasting to the rest of the world in English and seven foreign languages – Afrikaans, Arabic, French, German, Italian, Portuguese and Spanish, the last two to both Europe and Latin America. When the war ended it was using more than forty languages, some of them directed to more than one part of the world (e.g. French to South-East Asia and Canada as well as to France). It had been a source of hope and inspiration to millions of people in Nazi-occupied Europe and had actively helped the resistance movements. Its prestige, like that of Britain herself, was at a peak. It had acquired a reputation for honesty and was acknowledged as the foremost broadcasting organisation in the world, in quality as well as quantity.

This was a considerable achievement, and it does not detract from it to point out that it was to a large extent due to the fortunes of war. Britain was the only effective opponent of the Axis powers for a year; as a result she became a symbol of resistance to those who

had succumbed. The only contacts they had with this symbol were in some areas the RAF and everywhere the BBC. As the Prime Minister of Belgium put it after the war: 'The BBC renewed our confidence and forged our courage.'

So far no revisionist historian has claimed that the world would be a better place if the Nazis had won the war, and it can still be seen as a fight between qualified good and undeniable evil. 'It is the evil things we shall be fighting against,' Neville Chamberlain said in his broadcast on 3 September, and most people in most parts of the world agreed with him. So the BBC acquired a moral advantage which was of great help, particularly when speaking to the people of occupied Europe.

But this was to come later. In the first months of the war, when there was little British military activity, it was the German radio which made the running. William Joyce, nicknamed Lord Haw-Haw by an ingenious journalist, had a large audience for his propaganda broadcasts in English. He was seen as a joke, but behind the laughter was an unwilling acknowledgement that perhaps there was something in what he said, particularly when he spoke of social conditions in Britain.

The BBC had nothing to compare with Haw-Haw. In fact, the British, thought by Hitler to be so good at propaganda, made a sorry mess of it in the early part of the war.

A Ministry of Information was established, but its responsibilities and its relationship with the other ministries were ill-defined. It became a graveyard for the reputation of several ministers, including Reith himself, until Brendan Bracken, a protégé of Churchill, came to it in 1941 and carried out a sweeping re-organisation. Nor were relations between the BBC and the government harmonious; at one time Churchill referred to the corporation as 'an enemy within the gates.' (Things don't change much.) The trouble was that the BBC seemed always to be reporting bad news and thus damaging morale. But the fact was that for a long time there was usually only bad news to report – one defeat after another until El Alamein in November 1942.

American-born William Joyce, 'Lord Haw-Haw', broadcast for the Nazis from 1939. After the war he was tried in England for treason on the grounds that, as holder of a British passport, his allegiance was to Britain. He was found guilty and hanged in 1946.

Hugh Greene, who was in charge of broadcasts to Germany from the autumn of 1940 until after the end of the war, later commented that there was no doubt about the correct policy – to tell the truth consistently and frankly, and determined never to play down a disaster. 'We were not in fact being merely quixotic in following a policy of telling the truth. If we were right to foresee a long war the time was bound to come when the tide would turn and we should have victories to report. The audience in Germany and in the German forces, having heard us talk frankly about our defeats, would believe us when we talked about our victories, and the will to resist in a hopeless situation could, one hoped, be effectively undermined.' (*The Third Floor Front*, by Sir Hugh Greene, The Bodley Head, 1969)

This needs some qualification. In wartime the media do not tell the whole truth – patriotism and censorship see to that. Nor did the policy of not concealing disasters spring fully-armed from the ground in the German service in 1940. It applied throughout the BBC and was inherent in the philosophy Reith had fostered from the earliest days. It was difficult to maintain when there seemed to be nothing but disasters, and at times it infuriated the government, but it finally proved its worth. The tide did eventually turn, and there were victories to report. It was almost as if the BBC had written the script so that events would coincide with its philosophy.

The script, though, began badly. During the Norwegian campaign, in the spring of 1940, BBC reports were over-optimistic. It carried false reports of British successes emanating from neutral Sweden.

Unlike the newspapers, it was not given advance inform-ation that the British were to evacuate Norway – apparently to deceive the enemy. As a result it buoyed up the hopes of listeners who were all the more

In October, 1940, a delayed-action bomb killed seven people, injured many others and blew out part of the west side of Broadcasting House. Listeners to the nine o'clock news heard the announcer pause, and then continue.

shaken when the withdrawal took place.

There was a similar sad tale when the Germans turned their attention to Holland, Belgium, Luxembourg and France in May 1940. They swept through to the Channel, trapping the British army which had to be rescued from Dunkirk. This time the fault was that of the French military authorities. Their communiqués were Panglossian – 'strategic withdrawals to prepared positions', 'heavy enemy losses', 'brilliant counter-attacks', 'confidence prevails' and so on – so that when the collapse became too obvious to be concealed any longer the public felt betrayed.

With the French surrender the 'phoney war' was finally over and the 'finest hour' was at hand. For the BBC it became a time of unprecedented expansion in broadcasting abroad. New transmitters were ordered – some from the United States – and more staff were recruited; the numbers employed in broadcasting overseas went up by more than five hundred per cent in the first eighteen months of the war.

Although the government had decreed the expansion it offered little help in solving the problems it created – for example, where to put all these extra people. In December 1940 a land mine caused so much damage to Broadcasting House that the European services had to be moved to a disused skating rink in Maida Vale – with a glass roof. This was hardly the best place to be when London was being bombed every night and after a good deal of difficulty a new home was found for them. This was in Bush House, where there were already some basement studios (used by a commercial firm) and offices. Bush House was built in the late nineteen-twenties by a Mr. Irving T. Bush of the Bush Terminal Company of New York, and was dedicated to the friendship of the English-speaking peoples, as a notice above the main entrance still proclaims. After the war all broadcasts abroad, not just those to Europe,

were concentrated there and an increasingly large part occupied by the BBC, which however, never owned it. A fuller account of the history of the building is given in the Appendix.

During the war it was once described in Parliament as 'the black hole of Tooting Bec' (for security reasons its real position was not revealed). It was badly ventilated, stuffy and overcrowded, but according to Hugh Greene, 'it was a curiously cheerful atmosphere in which we worked; we had a lot of fun.' The new services to Europe had brought in people of many nationalities – actors, film or theatre directors, academics, journalists. They regarded the BBC as a very stuffy organisation. In Hugh Greene's words: 'When a BBC administrator descended on Bush House we tended to regard him as a strange thing from outer space; he came from a different world.'

The BBC went to some lengths to ensure that its new broadcasters did not become security risks. Language supervisors, British nationals with linguistic skills, were attached to the various sections to ensure accurate translations from English. During transmissions they had authority to switch off temporarily. This power was used from time to time to correct a mistake, but it is a mark of the integrity of the staff that it never had to be used for reasons of security.

A BBC paper from 1940 shows the difficult position it faced in broadcasting to Europe at a time when the Nazis controlled the radio stations. 'The countries of Europe are now subjected to a drum fire of broadcast propaganda in their languages from stations which speak with a single inspiration but through skilfully specialised channels,' it said.

To counteract this, greater attention was now paid to the needs and tastes of individual countries and individual groups in these countries. The staple diet of news and talks was supplemented by other types of programme, such as discussion groups and dramatised documentaries. The paper put

*The inventor of the 'V' sign, Victor de Lavelaye,
(left), with the editor of the BBC Belgian service,
Professor Nand Geersens, in 1944.*

stress on the need to have a clear idea of the
different types of listeners. It went on:
'Scandinavians do not need to be told what
democracy is, but before they will accept us
as the leaders of the New Europe, they want
some answer to the plausible attacks made
on our social conditions by the Germans;
Spaniards and Portuguese require to be
satisfied that with us democracy does not
mean municipal corruption; Germans and
Italians require education in the very meaning of the word.

Again, the Dutch housewife who listens
to a programme at 10 am while she is doing
the housework needs different fare from her
son, who stays up until 1 am in the hope of
hearing a youth programme which will
support him in organising passive resistance
to the Germans.'

One campaign which came to be directed
at all European listeners was 'V for Victory'
which began in 1941. It was the brainchild
of the Belgian programme organiser, who
noted that V was the initial letter of *Victoire*
in French and *Vrijheid* (Freedom) in Flemish,
so encompassing both the languages of

Belgium. He began using it as a morale
booster, urging Belgians to go out and chalk
up V signs wherever they could – on walls,
doorways and other suitable surfaces. Soon it
became popular in Holland and Northern
France as well. The campaign was then taken
up by other European services and a 'V'
committee and spokesman appointed, to
broadcast in the English service to Europe.
He was known as Colonel Britton; actually
he was the assistant news editor, Douglas
Ritchie, but the sense of drama surrounding
the campaign was heightened by the fact
that his true identity was kept secret.

In an extraordinary publicity coup an
American reporter, granted an interview
with him, had to be content with talking to
a man who remained hidden behind a
partition.

The Morse signal for V, three dots and a
dash, has the same rhythm as the opening
notes of Beethoven's Fifth Symphony, so
Beethoven was brought into the act. The
notes played on the timpani were introduced
as the station identification for all the
services to Europe. Colonel Britton suggested
a variety of ways for using the sound in
ordinary life – a schoolmistress clapping her
hands to call her pupils, for instance,
customers calling to the waiters in a cafe.
There were reports of V signs appearing on
walls and buildings from nations as far apart
as Norway and Greece. Winston Churchill
gave the campaign a boost by adopting the V
sign and describing it in a special message as
'the symbol of the unconquerable will of the
people of the occupied territories.'

Colonel Britton announced the
mobilisation of the 'V' army, but, of course,
there was no such army, and the occasion
was an anti-climax. The campaign suffered
from the fact that it was not part of any
planned strategy to prepare for a military
assault but an isolated morale booster,
created by chance. It stirred peoples'
imaginations – but that does not win wars.

It had its opponents at the time, and after the war they argued that it was an irrelevant exercise which may have cost unnecessary lives.

However, the Germans took it seriously enough to claim it for themselves, with limited success. On the grounds that V stood for victory against Bolshevism (*Viktoria*) they erected their own signs. For example, in Brussels there was a notice announcing: 'V means German victory on all fronts.' The effect was spoiled by a small boy who wrote under it: 'V means Jackie's birthday tomorrow.' Nazi-controlled radio stations also began to broadcast the opening bars of Beethoven's Fifth Symphony on the reasonable grounds that Beethoven was German and so making it the most frequently-played snatch of music of the whole war.

The last broadcast by Colonel Britton was in May 1942, when he explained that he would not speak again until 'the moment comes to indicate a particular line of action which is needed.' The moment never came.

Resistance to the Germans was becoming organised and a Special Operations Executive had been set up to encourage and supply the resistance groups springing up all over Europe. There was no room for the free-lance activities of the BBC, not tied to actual operational needs, and

the 'V' campaign was brought to an end.

The BBC itself was by now receiving more formal government guidance from a Political Warfare Executive, set up in 1941 . As in most matters involving the government and the foreign language services, the relationship between the PWE and the corporation remained fuzzy round the edges. The Executive could consult and advise. For example, on 26 November 1942 one of its weekly directives, three and a half foolscap pages of closely typed material, made the point that this had been the month that changed the war (a reference to the

'The Secret Hope', an E.H. Shepard drawing from 'Punch' published in 1942.

A grave Winston Churchill leaving Downing Street with Brendan Bracken, Minister of Information, in June, 1940.

Russian victory at Stalingrad and the British victory at El Alamein). 'Political warfare,' it said, ' will lose its great opportunity if it fails, when commenting on the military situation, to show that the military collaboration between Britain, Russia and America is a precursor of the same combined purpose in peace.'

However, the basis of the broadcasts was news, and news does not happen just once a week. In its bulletins and news talks the BBC was able to respond to events as they happened without close supervision, although like the press generally it was subject to voluntary censorship.

The PWE had regional sections which were in touch with the appropriate language services, but the degree of control they exercised depended very much on individual personalities. In any case, editors of the larger sections, such as the French and German, sought to assert their independence from the central newsroom, often re-writing news stories and ignoring newsroom directives, adding an air of what the BBC

likes to describe as 'creative tension' – in other words, conflict.

As the war progressed, the European services came to contribute directly to the struggle by broadcasting code messages to resistance groups. The messages were provided by the SOE and were usually either to confirm that an operation was to take place or to delay or cancel it. They were broadcast for several days before the operation was due and for some days after its completion or cancellation, so that no one message could be associated with a particular operation. Sometimes they were acknowledgements of the safe arrival in Britain of people or documents or warnings of danger.

The BBC staff who transmitted them were aware, of course, that they were going to resistance groups, but they did not know what the messages meant. Sometimes they resented their number. The French service, which received the bulk of them, once complained of having to transmit 20 lines of messages in a bulletin of only ten minutes.

42

Sometimes, too, they led to perplexity. A 1942 message said: 'Courvoisier, nous vous rendons visite' and was reported by someone who heard it to the head of the brandy firm, then living in England. He asked the BBC for further details, as did a Mrs. Courvoisier, who asked if it meant that her children were on their way to England from France. They were both told that the use of the name was a coincidence and that it was impossible for security reasons to give any more information.

In 1942 the BBC began to broadcast in Morse code in the early hours of the morning. The idea was to help clandestine newspapers, which were beginning to appear in most of the occupied countries. Half an hour of news was provided, every word repeated, in English, French and German. A Norwegian who escaped to England described in a broadcast how these newspapers were produced:

'In a cellar somewhere in my snow-covered country a girl is crouching in front of a muffled loudspeaker taking shorthand notes of the BBC news. In his lodgings a student is typing the stencils for to-morrow's *Radio Post*. In a boathouse a young factory worker turns the handle of the duplicator. In a deserted office three young clerks are pinning the sheets together, folding the finished papers and putting them into the envelopes... Hundreds and hundreds of people are at work producing and distributing the illegal papers in my country, and before midday to-morrow their duplicated papers, bringing the latest war news, will have covered the greater part of Norway.'

Morse was replaced in 1944 by ordinary speech transmissions, but a transcript of one of the last Morse bulletins has been retained in the BBC archives. It begins: 'VVV Stalin announces annihilation Hun Eighth Army trapped Korsun pocket fifty-two thousand Huns killed eleven thousand taken prisoner all Hun equipment captured...'

Not all broadcasts to Europe were the responsibility of the BBC. There were 'black' radio stations, purporting to operate from inside Germany itself, which were under the auspices of the PWE and regarded with distaste by the purists of the BBC. After the United States entered the war it set up its own foreign broadcasting service under the Office of War Information, the precursor of the Voice of America, which used BBC transmitters to relay programmes to Europe.

A different form of collaboration enabled certain European governments to produce their own programmes as an addition to those of the BBC. The Dutch, the French and the Poles were among them. Although nominally independent, they were required to submit scripts in advance for reasons of policy, and this led to frequent rows. A cross memorandum written in September 1942 by the then Controller of European Services, Sir Ivone Kirkpatrick (who had come to the BBC from the Foreign Office), summed up the problem. Referring to the Free (later the Fighting) French, he complained: 'If our control is excessively rigid there is a row with the Free French headquarters which is apt to lead to a remonstrance from the Foreign Office. If our control is not rigid enough we are liable to be censured by British authorities outside the Foreign Office.' This was bad enough, but there was worse. The Poles were 'constantly attempting to misuse their liberty in order to put over material which is definitely embarrassing to us' and, as for the Yugloslavs, their govern-ment was not only 'quite incompetent but rent by dissensions, Serbs, Croats and Slovenes all quarrelling among themselves.'

All the services, in fact, had problems of their own. In the next two chapters we shall look briefly at each of them to see how they responded to the needs of their listeners and instilled a belief in a final Allied victory.

CHAPTER FOUR

To Friends and Enemies Alike

DURING the 'phoney war' the French service managed to gather to itself a nucleus of listeners attracted by the policy of not concealing bad news. One of the last letters the BBC received from France before the surrender expressed concern at an agreement between the ministers of information of the two countries because 'we are afraid that your bulletins will lose much of their interest.'

Queen Elizabeth, now the Queen Mother, broadcast to the women of France during this critical period, and just after the French surrender a new voice was heard – that of General de Gaulle. His first broadcast is part of history, but few people in France seem to have heard it at the time, and it has become famous only in retrospect.

De Gaulle was in London as a minister in the government of M. Paul Reynaud, who was superseded by Marshal Petain. He wanted to broadcast an appeal for Frenchmen to continue the fight. The British government still had some hope that resistance might continue from French overseas territories, so the Cabinet, meeting without Churchill, at first refused permission. But, after more consultation among ministers, permission was eventually granted. The decision was made late, and there was no opportunity to rehearse the broadcast.

Elisabeth Barker (who became diplomatic correspondent at Bush House after the war) was present. Many years later she recalled that when he arrived at Broadcasting House De Gaulle was silent and pre-occupied until his time came. He addressed himself to French soldiers still in Britain, having been evacuated through Dunkirk, and asked them to communicate with him. 'The flames of French resistance must not be extinguished, *will* not be extinguished', he declared.

De Gaulle broadcast a number of times after that, and it was through radio that he became well-known to his fellow-countrymen. He was described by Cecilia Gillie of the French service as the ideal broadcaster: 'He arrived on time with a well-prepared script. I do not remember ever hearing him fluff. He was courteous and always found time to thank the recording engineer after he had finished.'

De Gaulle reserved himself for major occasions. For everyday broadcasts he appointed a spokesman, Maurice Schumann, a former journalist who was later to become

To help prepare for the Allied invasion of Europe it was important to step up the war of words. Here, in June 1943, Donald Edwards, European News Editor, receives news flashes and relays them

his country's foreign minister. Schumann had a high-pitched voice, particularly when excited. To remedy this the BBC staff tactfully told him that his words would penetrate jamming more easily if he pitched them as low as possible. In this way he became an effective broadcaster on the official Free French programme, known as *Honneur et Patrie*.

Another famous broadcaster on the French service was Winston Churchill himself. Just before the French surrender Churchill had made an offer of union between the two countries, and in October 1940 he spoke directly to the French people in their own language. He was helped to prepare his talk by one of the many talented Frenchmen who came to work for the BBC after the French collapse, Michel Saint-Denis, who broadcast under the name of Jacques Duchesne.

Saint-Denis was a theatre director who had worked in Britain before the war and became a liaison officer with the British Expeditionary Force. He and Churchill spent most of the day together, 'emptying as they worked a bottle of brandy' according to Cecilia Gillie. Churchill's instructions were that the translation from English should not be too correct: 'I want to be understood as I am.' Saint-Denis himself was moved almost to tears by Churchill's concern for France, and the simple opening statement growled over the air in that distinctive voice still has the power to move: 'Français, prenez garde, c'est moi, Churchill qui vous parle.'

Most members of the French service joined after Dunkirk, and few had previous experience of broadcasting. But with their British colleagues they produced programmes which had a brilliance all their own. From occupied France itself came a complaint that

General de Gaulle at the BBC microphone in 1940. Leader of the Free French, and a frequent broadcaster, he became President of the Fifth Republic in December, 1958.

'the very soul of French wit has fled to London.' They produced parodies of popular songs and anti-German jingles, for example:

> Depuis Strasbourg jusqu'à Biarritz
> La radio est aux mains de Fritz

and

> Radio Paris ment
> Radio Paris ment
> Radio Paris est Allemand

Many were recruited by Saint-Denis, and they set about discussion programmes in an original way. In one programme they had a sort of licensed pessimist who would say (what many Frenchmen were thinking early in the war) that there was no prospect of victory; then there would be an argument in which the others taking part tried to convince him he was wrong. *Les Français Parlent aux Français* was what it said, a half hour of informal discussion by Frenchmen in London for Frenchmen in France.

Tangye Lean, who worked in Bush House (and became Director of External Broadcasting after the war) described Saint-Denis and his programmes in these terms: 'With a message to give and enough theatrical experience to invent original ways of giving it, half an hour's propaganda became more exciting in his hands than any other radio programme I had heard. Neither content nor means of presentation gave the listener a chance to switch off; themes were attacked from all angles, angrily, wittily, musically, in dialogue...' (*Voices in the Darkness*, Secker and Warburg, 1943)

The allied landings in North Africa in 1942 raised hopes in France but also led to a crisis in the French service. The allies had decided to treat with Admiral Darlan, regarded as a supporter of the Vichy regime, rather than with de Gaulle, whom the Americans disliked. The Foreign Office vetoed two broadcasts de Gaulle had planned on the subject, and in fury, the Free French

retaliated by refusing any co-operation with the service. The crisis was resolved when Darlan was assassinated on Christmas Eve, but it foreshadowed the political disputes that were to emerge in France after the war.

As D-Day approached the French service became increasingly a channel of communication from the allies to the people of France. There was advice about leaving the towns for the country, for instance, or about forming groups of friends for mutual help and protection. The country was being prepared for invasion, and the number of operational code messages rose until on 4 June, two days before the Normandy landings, they lasted for twenty minutes. The resistance groups were being given their instructions for D-Day.

On the day itself the BBC broadcast messages from such dignitaries as the King of Norway, the Grand Duchess of Luxembourg, the Queen of the Netherlands, the Prime Minister of Belgium and General Eisenhower, the allied supreme commander. The list did not include de Gaulle. He had not been consulted about the text of the proclamation from Eisenhower to the people of occupied Europe, a proclamation which put him at the end and made no mention of his claim to represent France.

So, although the other messages were transmitted on the morning of D-Day, de Gaulle, snubbed by his allies, stalked to Bush House, sealed off from the public for security reasons, to broadcast his own message for transmission at midday.

Within months of D-Day, with France freed, the French service had ended its wartime task. It made what was described as its worst mistake in the four years of German occupation when it reported the liberation of Paris several days before it actually happened; it was misled by a communiqué from the resistance in the capital. But this did not nullify its achievements.

It received many tributes from official and private sources – four thousand letters in

December 1944 alone. The message of all of them was essentially the same: 'When everything looked black and hopeless listening to the BBC became the day's ration of courage and confidence'.

The object of the German service, of course, was just the opposite – to sap courage and confidence. In the early days of the war this was no more than a distant dream; after all, the Germans were winning. In fact, there was a crisis of confidence in the service itself in 1940.

The German staff were by definition anti-Nazi – many were Jewish – and Nazi victories on the mainland of Europe made them apprehensive. At the same time there was a campaign in Britain against enemy aliens, with many being interned, and it is hardly surprising that morale was low. It was not improved by the policy of using Germans only as translators or anonymous voices.

The named commentators were British, with the exception of the exiled German author Thomas Mann who recorded a regular commentary from his home in the United States.

There were good reasons for this policy. Anonymity offered some protection for broadcasters regarded as traitors in their own homeland. More importantly, perhaps, the BBC could not afford to be seen as a station run by Jewish émigrés; it had to be clearly British. But the German staff complained they were made to feel like second-class citizens.

The service was hampered by the lack of a clear statement of aims by the British government. The other European services could hold out to their listeners the prospect of liberation. The British had originally made a distinction between the German people and their Nazi leaders, but this did not last long. Most Germans supported the Nazis, at least passively, and as the war became more brutal the distinction disappeared. The allies finally came up with

the doctrine of unconditional surrender – a gift to German propagandists, since it enabled them to claim with some justification that the very life of their country was at stake.

The German service had a habit of rejecting Hitler's offers of peace even before the government. Maurice Latey, who was to become a distinguished commentator after the war, did just that when he had been with the BBC for no more than six months.

After Poland had been conquered in the autumn of 1939 Hitler offered to make peace with Britain and France. Maurice Latey immediately wrote a commentary pouring scorn on the offer.

In a booklet marking the 50th anniversary of the German service he recalled: 'I woke next morning to press headlines announcing 'BBC rejects Hitler peace offer' before the government had time to consider it. I approached the office next morning in fear and trembling only to find on my desk a note from my boss, which I still cherish, congratulating me on my effort.'

There was another peace offer the following year, after the fall of France. This time there was a discussion about how (not whether) it should be rejected. Sefton Delmer, former *Daily Express* correspondent in Berlin, who knew Hitler personally, delivered the reply: 'Let me tell you what we here in Britain think of this appeal of yours to what you are pleased to call our reason and common sense. Herr Fuhrer and Reichskanzler, we hurl it right back at you, right in your evil-smelling teeth.' Leonard Miall, who was also to have a distinguished BBC career, commented: 'The effect was electric. Extracts from the broadcast were printed around the world, alongside Hitler's speech. And in Germany itself there was consternation.' Three days later the government formally rejected the peace offer.

In 1941 the German service was expanded and reorganised. It developed programmes aimed at different sections of society. There was a programme for workers in the early morning, jazz (condemned as decadent by Hitler and banned in Germany) and dance music and programmes for the forces which included details of prisoners of war. A special transmission for Austria was introduced.

Evidence that some Germans listened came at first from captured sailors or airmen. Among them were the crew of a U-boat whose captain happened, oddly enough, to be a communist.

Hugh Greene later recalled: 'He was rather an amusing character. Dick Crossman and I took him out to lunch at the Reform Club. I often wonder what the members of the club would have thought if they had known that there was a communist U-boat prisoner of war among them.' The U-boat captain said he personally thought the programmes for workers were rather dull, but his father, an old socialist, liked them and there were millions like him.

Later in the war evidence of listening increased. An anonymous German wrote a long letter to the BBC in 1942 in the course of which he said: 'You keep the flame awake, you console the sometimes despairing, you strengthen the weak who more and more thought they must resign themselves because of the so-called victories; you prevent the light of the day's truths and of the eternal truths from going under in the German people.'

And by early 1944 it was reported by a French student escaped from occupied Brittany: 'Almost all Germans listen to the BBC's *Hier ist England*. No death penalties are imposed because it would entail most of the Wehrmacht's demise.'

The service made effective use of Hitler's speeches, recording them, then broadcasting extracts back to Germany when what he said had been falsified by events. For example, Hitler was heard predicting the immediate defeat of Britain. That, the commentator

said sarcastically, was eighteen months ago. One programme was built up almost entirely of records of Hitler. It took the form of a conversation – an Englishman asking questions and receiving two contradictory answers, in each case extracted from a speech.

Another telling piece of propaganda was a commentary on Goebbel's weekly article in the periodical *Das Reich*, broadcast before the article actually appeared. How this was done remained a mystery to the Germans until the end of the war, but the explanation was simple. Berlin sent an advance copy of the text to the German authorities in Norway by Hellschreiber – the German tape machine. It was picked up by the BBC monitoring service and transmitted to Bush House.

Dramatised features, usually with a satirical bent, were favoured by the German service. As an example of their flavour here are a few lines from Kurt and Willi, one of the most popular and a favourite of the future Chancellor Adenauer. Kurt is a naive schoolmaster, Willi a member of the Ministry of Propaganda, and they meet regularly for a drink at a cafe in the Potsdamer Platz in Berlin:

WILLI: Heil Hitler, Kurt, sit down, the brandy is waiting.
KURT: Heil Hitler, Willi, sorry I'm late. It was the greengrocer, she was complaining that she had no vegetables and why was that? The papers had said there would be plenty of vegetables this summer – a high tide of vegetables. Usual grumbles by women. I had to give her a lecture.
WILLI: Dear me, Kurt, you ought to be in my profession; you are a born propagandist. But tell me, how did you explain away this shortage of vegetables to the poor woman?
KURT: I said there was no real lack; the actual reason is the lack of transport, and that our transport must be used in the first place for our troops in the east to supply

them with everything. This must be understood by every good German. It's the shortage of wagons.

WILLI: And the ships.

KURT: Ships? Why, what have the ships to do with it?

WILLI: Quite a lot, my dear Kurt. The fact is that Germany is almost as dependent on shipping as England. But we propagandists take great care not to mention it.

KURT: I don't get you, Willi. Ships? We are not an island.

WILLI: Nevertheless in peacetime a large part of our transport was by water. When our ships are sunk, naturally our railways can't hope to cope with the overburden and strain.

KURT: But I didn't know our ships were being sunk.

WILLI: I bet you didn't. There are lots of things between heaven and earth – or sky and water – which you don't know and we propagandists keep absolutely mum about.

KURT: Anyway, I am glad the English are worse off than we are. They must be nearly starving. By the way, I'm surprised your propagandists don't make more of that point.

WILLI: We told the press to pipe down on this, too.

KURT: For heaven's sake, why?

WILLI: Because you see if we go on saying truly and honestly that the English are starving, next year people will want to know why they are still alive and fighting...

The last conversation between Kurt and Willi was broadcast in April 1945. It ended with Willi saying to Kurt: 'I must go out now and see if there is any news.' There was. Immediately the programme was over it was announced that Hitler was dead.

A VERY NAUGHTY CARTOON

B.B.C.
FOREIGN
PROPAGANDA
STUDIO

SILENCE!

– MARCHY –

" —and so we call upon the occupied countries to rise against their oppressors—with the exception of India, of course!"

Even in the gloomy days of 1943 it was possible for cartoonists to take a wry look at British foreign-language broadcasts.

Broadcasting to the second member of the Axis, Italy, presented a different set of problems. Mussolini remained neutral until just before the fall of France and even after he had declared war was never taken as seriously as the Nazis. In fact, in July 1940 the Foreign Office felt it necessary to make a strong request to the BBC not to jeer at Italy. However, Italian defeats in the Western desert towards the end of that year resulted in an item which read: 'Information from north Europe says a new dance is coming into vogue in many European capitals. It is called Toscana or Tuscany Wolf Dance and has been dedicated to the brave Italian nation. It is an easy dance to learn – one step forward and three steps backward.'

At the time the British were grateful for any victories, but the childish humour of this

A 1945 photograph
of Colonel Stevens,
who broadcast
regularly to Italy,
from 1939 onwards.

item does not perhaps represent the BBC at its best.

Italian exiles played a larger part in broadcasting to their own country than their German colleagues. But the most popular speaker was an Englishman, Colonel Stevens. He had been military attaché in Rome and had two sisters married to Italians, with sons in the Italian armed forces.

He began his news commentaries in 1939, when Italy was still neutral, at first weekly, later four times a week, and won a huge following. He was careful to distinguish between the Italian people and the Fascist regime and blamed the misfortunes of the former on the latter. For example: 'Mussolini must have known that the war was lost for Italy before even embarking on it. It was lost on the cornfields. The battle of the grain has been fought for the past ten years under the orders of Mussolini, who urged it on with words, words, words. He sowed not grain but wind, and now he reaps the whirlwind.'

In 1941 Colonel Stevens was reported by

a traveller from the north of the country to be 'the most popular figure in all Italy.' This was perhaps an exaggeration, but he became widely known as Colonello Buonasera from his habit of signing off his talks, and one listener wrote: '...we all rush to the set and when he says his "Buon giorno or Buona sera" we all answer in chorus: "Buona sera, Colonello"'. When allied troops landed in Sicily in 1943 they were puzzled to find among the welcome signs scrawled in one small town 'Viva Stevens' – a gentleman few had heard of.

Another popular commentator on the Italian service was known as Candidus – in reality John Marus, born in London of Italian parents but educated in Italy and imprisoned there for a time for anti-fascist activities. There were feature programmes, one of which consisted of a dialogue between a German and an Italian businessman. It was used to make sly attacks on German attitudes. There were musical programmes, too, and interviews with artists who had a message. The first of these early in 1941 was with an Italian tenor who had left his country in disgust at Fascism.

The task of the service changed radically in 1943. Mussolini fell in July, and a few months later the government which succeeded him surrendered to the allies. German troops quickly occupied the north and centre of the country, and the allies had to fight a long, bitter campaign through Italy. In the days just after the surrender, when newspapers and the Italian radio were suspended, listening to the BBC reached a peak. Then (in the words of the *BBC Yearbook for 1944*) 'the great objective was the re-birth of a fighting spirit in a country which had changed from being an enemy to a co-belligerent.' The BBC sent messages to the partisans who had taken up arms against the Germans and gave instructions to factory workers in the industrial north on the best way to cause obstruction.

The immense prestige BBC broadcasts had won meant that more Italians listened to them than to all other foreign transmissions put together, more indeed than to their own German-controlled service. Although the German authorities often threatened punishment for listening they never imposed the death penalty. Perhaps, said the *BBC Yearbook* at the time, they shrank from the task of shooting an entire nation.

There was another task the Italian service was called upon to perform. The British ambassador argued that the great difficulty was to combat the Russian and Italian Communist Party propaganda which made its principal appeal to the working classes, best reached by radio. 'It is essential,' he wrote in a telegram, 'that these classes be kept adequately informed on British affairs and the British way of life if, as seems likely, they are going to be a considerable element in the internal political re-organisation of Italy.' As so often happens, the ambassador was knocking at an open door. The BBC had begun a programme for Italian workers in 1943 – without indulging in the class war – and after the armistice turned its attention increasingly in all the European services to what became known as 'Projection of Britain', a soft-sell approach to the task of winning friends and influencing people.

CHAPTER FIVE

Intellectual Invasion of the Continent

DURING THE WAR, Italy was in the curious position of being a partially-occupied country. To each of those which were completely occupied the BBC spoke in its own language.

There was a Dutch service broadcasting to Holland and, from 1944, the then Dutch East Indies. The Netherlands government had, as already mentioned, its own transmission, Radio Oranje, which was allowed a good deal of freedom. Queen Wilhelmina and Prince Bernhard often broadcast to their people and, although the Nazis once tried to confiscate all the radio sets in the country, listening to London was widespread.

A service to Belgium broadcast in French and Flemish, but it was entirely under the control of the BBC until 1943, when the Belgian government was given two fifteen-minute transmissions a day, one in each language. From late 1940 there was a transmission in what was known as Luxembourg patois, at first five minutes a week, later fifteen minutes a day.

Each of the Nordic countries presented a different problem. Finland had to fight off a Russian attack in the winter of 1939/40 and joined Hitler in his attack on Russia in June

1941. It was therefore classed as an Axis satellite, and the task of the BBC was seen as trying to detach it from Germany. This, of course, was never likely to be achieved, but its following was indicated by a comment made in 1944 by a Finnish member of Parliament who said he knew one old lady who 'only believes in the Bible and British broadcasts.'

Sweden remained neutral throughout the war. It had a free and effective press, so Swedes were able to take a detached view of the propaganda efforts of both sides. The Swedish service was therefore less polemical than others. It had a higher proportion of cultural items and projections of Britain. It presented talks by eleven Nobel prizewinners – Einstein and Thomas Mann among them – and attracted a fair-sized audience.

In Norway the BBC at first had problems of credibility because of its over-optimism during the military campaign of 1940. It was accused of having put out 'fake news' – 'just another form of propaganda.' The Norwegian government and King Haakon escaped to London and so did several members of the broadcasting service. They were eventually seconded to the BBC at their own request and worked so successfully with their British colleagues that by 1941 a Norwegian who escaped to the United States was reporting: 'Nobody reads any newspapers or listens to any radio except the BBC.'

Two years later a letter to London from a Norwegian correspondent said: 'That the Norwegian people have held their stand so calmly and definitely is above all due to the BBC, for without it such a stand would have been unthinkable.'

Denmark presented a different situation again. The Danish government had not tried to resist the German takeover, and the country was officially described as 'a model protectorate' with business as usual.

But the occupation produced frictions. There were sporadic acts of resistance which were followed by strikes and demonstrations. Finally, the German army took over the running of the country. The BBC did not at first encourage resistance. But it did report the heroism shown in other occupied countries and in 1942 a Danish political leader who had escaped to Britain broadcast a call for action over the Danish service.

From then on Danes regarded themselves at war and the BBC was with them. From pro-Nazi newspapers came complaints of broadcasts 'spreading poison and incitement in thousands of Danish homes.' Later some Danes were to complain that the service was out of touch with popular feeling in the country and not making the best use of material made available to it, but there is no doubt that it played a significant part in Danish resistance.

The Polish service was perhaps the most fraught of all, mainly because of events in Poland itself. Britain and France had gone to war to fulfil their guarantee to Poland when Hitler invaded in September 1939.

But they did nothing to help, even when Nazi Germany and the Soviet Union occupied the whole country between them. Many Poles escaped to the West, the Middle East and even East Africa, and the Polish service began an 'agony column of the air' to help them locate their relations.

The Polish government in exile had its own radio programme which, as we saw earlier, often caused problems to the British

Crown Prince Olaf of Norway broadcasts in the Norwegian service of the BBC in 1941. Many European monarchs in exile used the BBC as a way of keeping in touch with their subjects.

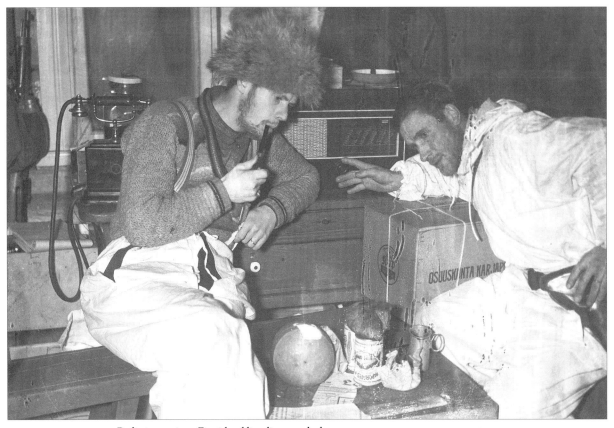

Radio in wartime: Finnish soldiers listen to the latest news.

authorities. Its broadcasts were carefully scrutinised, and the language supervisors (also known as switch censors) had orders to report even minor deviations from the script; to cut the programme off the air if necessary. The root of the problem was Polish mistrust of the Soviet Union, a distrust justified by events but inconvenient when applied to an important ally. For example, there was the massacre of Polish officers at Katyn, in the Soviet Union. This was officially blamed on the Nazis but believed by most Poles to be the work of the Russians. The Polish view is now known to have been true but at the time could not be publicly acknowledged by a British government conscious of the fact that it was the Red Army which was winning the war. The question of Poland's post-war frontiers and relations with the Soviet Union were also sources of dissension.

Then there was the Warsaw uprising of 1944. It lasted from 2 August to 5 October – 63 days – and cost the lives of 150,000 Poles. The Soviet army gave no help although it was nearby, being content to see the non-Communist leaders destroyed by the Germans. The BBC monitoring service was able to locate the radio station set up by the Home Army, responsible for the uprising, and broadcast its communiqués to the world. There was also direct communication by code from Warsaw. Towards the end, as German troops split the resistance groups from each other, communication between them was maintained by short wave transmissions via London. Just before the final surrender a spokesman for the Home Army thanked all those who had helped in the battle; among them was the head of the BBC Polish service.

Broadcasts to Czechoslovakia did not suffer from the same problems as those to Poland; relations with the Czechoslovak government in exile were described as 'harmonious'. The service had the advantage of possessing two outstanding statesman as speakers – President Benes and Jan Masaryk, a future foreign minister who was to die in mysterious circumstances in 1948. His first broadcast in 1939 announced: 'The hour of retribution is here.'

Listeners in Czechoslovakia took the BBC very seriously, and the service was cautious in calling for resistance. A broadcast in 1940 was misunderstood as a demand for immediate revolt and resulted in 60 workers being shot.

In the following year a call went out to boycott the press, and circulations fell dramatically. The German-controlled radio had to advertise the papers – for example, 'A terrible disaster has befallen the Swedish navy; details will be found in the newspapers.' The service once named a number of editors who were working with the Germans – and several of them promptly went down with food poisoning after a banquet. One of them later died, and the Czech radio accused the BBC of murdering him.

Although Czechoslovakia was liberated by the Soviet army, it was to London that people looked for guidance and support. An uprising in Slovakia in 1944 was planned by the exiled government in London; the BBC received communiqués from the spot in code and broadcast them within minutes. During the fighting which accompanied the liberation of Prague BBC bulletins were re-broadcast by the freed Czech radio. Soon after the end of the war there was a radio hook-up between Prague and London to celebrate.

The BBC service to Yugoslavia ran into problems as a result of the complex political scene there, and its role remained a matter of controversy after the war. The Axis powers invaded Yugoslavia in the spring of 1941, and the royalist government fled to London.

The first reports of resistance spoke of a group called the Chetniks under a General Mihailovic who supported the government and was, in fact, appointed Minister of War. But there was a rival, Communist, group, the Partisans, led by Tito. The BBC found it difficult to get reliable information about what was happening in the country.

A good deal came from government sources which naturally played up the role of Mihailovic. There was no way of checking it, and some of the BBC reports turned out to be inaccurate.

But the government's activities were more sinister than simply providing false information. Elisabeth Barker, who was in PWE at the time, recalled: 'The Yugoslav government had a weekly slot for young military officers to do military broadcasts. They were violently pro-Mihailovic young men who used to turn up at the last minute with scripts which were based on material they had from Mihailovic, awarding high honours to various of their colleagues for their gallantry.

It turned out that this meant gallantry in fighting the Partisans, but we didn't know this at the time.' There was worse. 'They used to read out names labelling them with the letter Z which, it was explained to us, meant merely moral condemnation. But apparently it really meant they were people Mihailovic didn't like and who were to be assassinated.'

The shocking fact that the BBC had been used – however unwittingly – to read out death lists rankled in Yugoslavia after the war.

As evidence accumulated that Mihailovic was collaborating with the Nazis, the British government shifted its support to Tito and in 1943 sent a military mission to the Partisans. By that time the BBC was able to monitor their communiqués, issued through the Soviet radio. They were found to be reasonably accurate, in spite of a tendency to exaggeration, so there was a rather more solid basis of information to go on. But even this did not stop mistakes. When Italy surrendered in 1943 there were still twenty Italian divisions in Yugoslavia. Chetniks and Partisans embarked on a race to take over the Italian-held part of the country. The situation became confused, and the BBC came in for criticism from both sides because, it was claimed, it had attributed successes to the wrong group.

The BBC service to Greece also had its share of troubles towards the end of the war. It had a considerable audience. A Greek who escaped in the summer of 1942 reported: 'Everyone listens to the BBC.' In the autumn of 1944 German troops withdrew from Greece because the advance of the Red Army threatened them with isolation.

The resistance movement was controlled by Communists, and Britain sent 60,000 troops to defeat them and set up a royalist government. In London there was strong criticism of this action in the press and a censure motion in Parliament. It was heavily defeated, but to Churchill's fury most Labour members abstained.

When the Greek service reported the criticism there were angry protests from the British military commander and the British ambassador, who happened to be Rex Leeper.

The government, in the shape of PWE, proposed that the service should confine itself to reporting official British and Greek communiqués and policy statements and British press comment which did not imply intervention in internal Greek affairs. J.B. Clark, then European controller, pointed out in a memo that this raised important issues of principle as well as practical difficulties –

J.B. Clark in 1945, deputy director of the BBC Overseas Services, whose principled attitude at the time was not entirely popular with Churchill, who had sent Allied troops to Greece to defeat the communists.

for example, if Greek affairs became a lively topic of discussion in the 'responsible' British press the Greek service would be unable to report the fact. Presumably, he added innocently, a government spokesman would take full responsibility for any consequent criticism of the BBC.

After this the proposal was dropped, but the problem posed by the incident was to recur. It is not difficult to understand the feelings of the people on the spot; they are carrying out government policy and, as they see it, being undermined by an organisation funded by the taxpayer. But the problem they are dealing with is a short-term one. In the long-term the BBC still has to go on broadcasting, and its credibility depends on its freedom to report facts which may be unpalatable to the government in power.

Another problem country was Spain, where the British ambassador was Sir Samuel Hoare, a pre-war government minister who had supported the policy of appeasing the dictators. At first he wanted the BBC to avoid all reference to the Spanish civil war which had only just ended. He succeeded in having one of the outstanding broadcasters on the Spanish service banned from the air for a time. Even Sir Ivone Kirkpatrick, with his Foreign Office background, eventually came to the conclusion that Hoare was being 'reckless and hysterical.'

Spain was neutral during the war, although Franco sent an army division to fight alongside the Germans in Russia. But this did not stop the authorities from jamming broadcasts or punishing people for possessing details of BBC programmes. All the same, there is

evidence that a good many people listened. A man from Catalonia wrote: 'I know of several persons whose entirely unfavourable views on an Allied victory have been changed as a result of BBC broadcasts.' Tangye Lean commented at the time that this statement was backed by so much similar evidence that the BBC could not be denied the credit for producing in Spain one of the clearest shifts of public opinion which took place in Europe.

Goebbels himself, the master Nazi propagandist, spoke of 'the intellectual invasion of the continent by the British radio.' This brief summary of the work of the men and women in the European services gives some idea of their extraordinary efforts. After a shaky start and faced with a huge preponderance of Nazi-controlled stations they waged a propaganda war and won it.

Radio propaganda was described at the time as being a fourth arm after the navy army, and air force, but experience has modified that view. There is no doubt about its value as a source of hope and inspiration to the people of Nazi-occupied Europe and an expression of confidence in ultimate victory which had an effect on opinion in enemy and neutral countries. It can have a certain value if it harnessed closely to military objectives. But wars have to be won by fighting. And what the last war showed was that if broadcasts are to be effective over a period they have to be credible.

Exaggerated claims and attempts to conceal bad news are fatal to credibility. But that does not stop people in high places arguing for them at times of crisis, even to-day.

CHAPTER SIX

Speaking to a World at War

IT WAS NOT just to Europe that the BBC spoke with a more powerful voice during the war. It developed its services to the rest of the world as well, less dramatically perhaps and not always with such effect, but with equally important implications for the future.

To start with, the foreign language services had been seen as an extension of the Empire Service and were all grouped together as the Overseas Services. In the winter of 1940/41 the government asked the BBC to prepare plans to treble its output abroad. There were all sort of difficulties and frustrations, but this was largely achieved. A large part of the expansion took place in the transmissions to Europe, so they were given a separate identity – European services – and those to the rest of the world became the Overseas Services, a distinction which still applies.

The basis of overseas broadcasting was the Empire Service which during the war lost that title, never to regain it. It became at various times the World Service in English, the Overseas Forces Programme, the General Forces Programme and the General Overseas Service. It developed several regional offshoots, including one to North America.

For the first two years of the war the United States was neutral. The German and Italian radios had been trying hard to sway American opinion, and at a time when Britain stood alone it was obviously important to counteract their influence. The Empire Service already had a transmission intended for the Western hemisphere, but its programmes were the same as those which went to the Empire as a whole, and no special effort was made to adapt them to a North American audience accustomed to a much slicker style of presentation.

In the summer of 1940 all that changed. The North American service is one of the more impressive of the BBC's achievements of the war, although comparatively little known. The Corporation went about it with thoroughness. It hired several Canadians to organise and present the new service, among them the actor Robert Beatty. It tightened up the presentation and arranged for first-class speakers to give commentaries. The service, it was announced, would include entertainment, a two-minute news summary, a commentary called 'Britain Speaks' and a new programme – a half-hour Radio Newsreel every night. This would broadcast 'political commentaries, eye-witness

One of the most ambitious projects of the BBC in 1942 was a series of programmes of news, talks, features and variety to North America. Interviews with ordinary people were popular – this one is in Trafalgar Square.

accounts of events in the news, short talks by soldiers, sailors and airmen – particularly Canadians – and civil defence workers.'

Radio Newsreel was an immediate success and was later extended to the other Overseas Services. It continued, cut down to quarter of an hour, in the World Service for many years, coming to an end only in 1991.

The new service was well received in Canada and the United States. Two weeks after it began *Time Magazine* was enthusing that it was 'a vast improvement over the stodgy stuff the the BBC used to shortwave to North America.

'With swing bands and torch singers, brisk news and political commentaries, "Britain Speaks" is at its best when novelist-playwright John Boynton Priestley holds forth.' Priestley, with his homely Yorkshire accent and homely Yorkshire views, was one of the regular speakers; he was popular on the domestic air as well. Others included the journalist Vernon Bartlett, the actors Leslie Howard and Robert Donat, the cartoonist David Low and the author Rose Macaulay, a cornucopia of talent.

One of the virtues of the service was that it brought war home to the Americans in a vivid and unforgettable manner. It was launched at a time when the Battle of Britain was in its preliminary stages, and one of the reports which caught the imagination of Americans was an account of an air battle over the Channel which was included in Radio Newsreel. It achieved a certain notoriety in Britain, where it was also heard, because it seemed to be using the techniques of a sports commentary to describe a life-and-death struggle:

In the early 1940s a number of studios at the BBC were used to make recordings of programmes so that they could be broadcast more than once.

'Someone's hit a German, and he's coming down in a long streak, coming down completely out of control, a long streak of smoke. He's going flat into the sea...there he goes! Splash! There's a terrific mix-up over the Channel! It's impossible to tell which are our machines and which are the Germans. There's a fight going on – you can hear the rattle of machine-gun bullets (heavy explosion). That was a bomb, as you may imagine. Here comes a Spitfire (machine-gun fire). There's another bomb dropping. It's dropped – it missed the convoy. You know they haven't hit the convoy in all this...'

The commentary, by Charles Gardner, ended: 'Well, that was really a hot little engagement while it lasted.'

The North American service gradually grew until by 1942 it was on the air for more than seven hours a day. By that time the United States was in the war, and there were programmes linking the American and Canadian forces in Britain with home. American programmes were transmitted to Britain via a BBC studio in New York.

Few people listened to the service on short waves. It was re-broadcast in Canada and by an increasing number of United States networks. On D-Day, the invasion of Normandy, no fewer than 725 out of 914 radio stations in the USA carried BBC War Reports. In the first half of 1945 regular re-broadcasting reached a peak. It was estimated that over 15 million people in the States were hearing one or more BBC programmes a week as the war in Europe drew to a close. Later in the year there was a marked decline; attention had shifted to the Pacific.

Towards the end of the war the BBC Press Office discovered an unusual listener, a Canadian government surveyor who took to his tent near the arctic circle when the first snows of autumn began to fall in August, 1944.

Having failed to pick up any American station, he twiddled the short wave knob and received the BBC loud and clear. He learned, among other things, that Paris had been liberated. He wrote to the BBC to tell them

That man again, Tommy Handley (left), with announcer Roy Rich in a variety programme for North America.

about it, adding (doubtless with his tongue firmly in his cheek) that the Indians liked to listen, but only when there were women singing and the Eskimos never listened except when they wanted to set their watches by Big Ben.

The service to the Western hemisphere was also intended for the West Indies and special programmes were devised for them. The first was in the summer of 1939, when a test match commentary was beamed there. As West Indian servicemen came to Britain to fight for her there were programmes linking them with the folks back home. By 1941 there were over four hours a week of special West Indian material in the North American service, a forerunner of what was to become a separate Caribbean service.

Services to other regions were developed. The Pacific service was intended for Australia, New Zealand and the Pacific islands, and a good deal of its material was re-broadcast by local stations. The African service included the programme in Afrikaans which had started just before the war and special programmes in English for colonial territories in East and West Africa. Through the peculiar geography which the BBC sometimes adopts for reasons of administrative convenience the African service also included programmes in Greek (for Cyprus) and Maltese.

Government influence over policy in English services was looser than it was in foreign languages. There was an Empire Division in the Ministry of Information, and the different government departments, such as the Dominions Office and the Colonial Office, had advice to tender.

But there was not the close relationship that developed between the Political Warfare Executive and the individual European services. Nor was it possible to create one. Broadcasting to a particular country in its own language was a very different matter from broadcasting in English to the world in general when it came to planning effective propaganda.

This did not provide protection from criticism from British diplomats, Members of Parliament and spokesmen of the fighting services. A note on policy and guidance in 1942 reflects some of the pressures: 'After the battle of Libya had taken a turn for the worse we set ourselves with the full concurrence of the military people at the Ministry of Information to raise no false hopes and paint a suitably sombre picture of the news.

This appeared to conflict with the desire of the British authorities in Cairo that our tone should be such as to hearten the troops and reassure the Egyptians. Here was a conflict between two conflicting (sic) considerations, each of which was clearly of major importance.' There was also a complaint from the Indian government 'saying we were overdoing our accounts of the work of the RAF in Egypt and a strongly worded complaint from the Air Ministry that we were giving far too little recognition to the work of the RAF in Egypt.'

There were other problems: 'The temptation to play safe by ignoring news at the request of one department or one territory sometimes has to be resisted, for safety from complaints in one area may be gained only at the expense of more complaints from other areas or at the expense of the efficiency and reputation of the service as a whole.'

The use of the word 'sometimes' in that extract shows how difficult it was for the BBC to retain some degree of independence during the war, beset as it was by competing interests.

The English service found itself increasingly catering for British forces abroad as the war itself expanded to other continents. It was amalgamated with the programme which went out to the forces at home to become the General Forces

Programme early in 1944, relinquishing the title in January 1947. A special entertainment unit was set up to produce programmes, many of them on discs to be re-broadcast by local forces stations.

Something of the flavour of the times is captured in this extract from a letter to the singer Anne Shelton from an army captain: 'Here we are in the desert, warlike, full of hate for the Hun, ready for war and you come and sing in 'Starlight'... Everything else goes into the background.'

Programmes were produced not just for the British but also for Dominion forces – for instance, 'Song time in the Laager' for the South Africans. There was even a special programme put on for the Libyan garrison of Tobruk, when the town was held for months behind the Axis lines.

The course of the war in North Africa had a considerable effect on the Arabic service, which was speaking to some of those most closely affected, notably in Egypt. In 1940 the service came in for strong criticism. Anthony Eden, then Secretary of State for War, toured the Middle East and in a telegram back to London said that wherever he went he heard complaints about BBC broadcasts, those in both English and Arabic: 'They are continually putting out rumours obviously emanating from enemy sources...In general BBC announcements show lack of virility and incisiveness...'

This was at a time when the reputation of the BBC with the government was at a low ebb. Ogilvie had not proved an effective director-general and was eventually replaced. The whole question of control of the BBC was discussed in Cabinet; a Cabinet committee was set up; there were more threats of a government takeover. In the end, in the usual British way, a compromise of a sort was reached with the creation of the Political Warfare Executive. But when the war took a turn for the better the complaints diminished anyway; the messenger was no

longer being blamed for the message.

When Allied troops drove the Axis powers out of North Africa and invaded Italy in 1943 the audience for the Arabic service increased. As the BBC *Handbook for 1944* put it: 'Our victories in the field were more eloquent than words in convincing a critical audience of the certainty of allied victory, and the battle of words was no longer the uphill struggle of 1941.' The handbook also detected a tendency 'albeit in a limited sense, for it to be looked upon as the national programme of Arabdom supplementing in a unique way the regional programmes of the different countries themselves.' This tendency was strengthened by the intro-duction of a fortnightly publication – the *Arabic Listener* – and an annual poetry competition which drew entries from all over the Middle East and beyond. It was an Arab listening in West Africa who paid the service one of its most fulsome tributes:

'Behold ! Your weekly programme schedule reaches me regularly – except when it is delayed in the post owing to the present war crisis brought about by that insubordinate house-painter, that insatiable and low-born tyrant, that manslayer, Hitler, may Allah destroy him and his adherents and grant humanity rest from his evil craft – a task easy unto Allah! Behold us here, constant auditors of your broadcasts, which are the greatest, the best arranged, the most richly expressed and most intelligible in language of all Arabic emissions!'

The Arabic transmissions became part of the Near East service during the war, together with broadcasts in Turkish and Persian. The Persian service began in 1940, and in the following year British troops moved into the country to forestall the Germans. Some of the Persian staff refused to collaborate on broadcasts, although they agreed to continue translating bulletins. The crisis was brought to an end when the Shah abdicated.

The 1942 'Radio Newsreel' control room, shortly before the popular, long-running programme goes on the air.

An enthusiastic journalist claimed that this was the first time a ruler had been toppled by radio. It was actually military and political action which produced the result, but the very fact that the BBC was reporting it cannot have been an insignificant factor. Broadcasting in Persian amounted to a few hours a week. In 1944 the hours were increased to make two daily transmissions. But it was found that hardly anybody could hear the second one because it was at a time when there was no electric power available, so it was dropped.

Broadcasting to India had its own particular problems. Indian nationalists, demanding complete independence, launched a 'Quit India' campaign against British rule in 1942, when there was a serious threat from Japan.

Their leaders were thrown into gaol, thus beginning a tradition under which Commonwealth leaders served an apprenticeship in prison before taking control of their countries. The Germans began broadcasting to India before the war, and the Japanese followed. Their broadcasts caused concern even before Japan entered the war. A Ministry of Information report at the beginning of 1941 commented on the 'violently anti-British propaganda' of transmissions to India which consistently publicised the movement for independence and made great use of the slogan: 'Asia for the Asians.'

Until the outbreak of war the government of India was not in favour of special BBC broadcasts to India beyond what was in the Empire service. It had its own All-India Radio which transmitted in the main Indian languages as well as English. But the war changed its mind; authority resided in London.

In 1939 an Indian Muslim, Z.A. Bokhari, of All-India Radio came to Britain to advise on publicity and immediately made his mark. He was a man of energy and enthusiasm; he became first director-general of Radio Pakistan after the war.

He argued in a policy paper that most Indians regarded the war as imperialist but at the same time were against Hitler. The object of propaganda, he said, must be to exploit this anti-Hitler feeling.

The BBC began broadcasting in Hindustani in May 1940 and later in several other Indian languages. It also developed a programme in English for India, produced by Bokhari.

This was aimed at Indian intellectuals and gave them the best of British culture. E.M. Forster, T.S. Eliot, V.S. Pritchett and Louis Macneice were among the contributors. George Orwell was another under his real name of Eric Blair; he was a producer as well as a speaker. He did not stay long, resigning in 1943 because he felt he was wasting both his time and public money.

One legacy of his career is the description of the canteen in the Ministry of Truth in his novel *Nineteen Eighty-Four*; it is said to be based on his memories of a BBC staff canteen.

In 1943 the service broadcast a series of round-table discussions on India's future – a bold gesture in the circumstances. Bokhari also invited British musicians to the studio to listen to Indian music, a foretaste of that fusion of styles that was to become popular in the sixties.

However, the ambivalence of British attitudes to India did not help. In 1941 Bokhari, in one of his trenchant memos. was complaining that if the British wanted to keep India in the Empire they would have to realise that 'it is wrong to allot ten hours and 13 minutes and 12 wavelengths a day to amuse the Sahib who has gone out to India from England and to devote only one hour and two wavelengths to convert Indian opinion.' (The Empire Service still regarded British expatriates as its main audience.)

In fairness to the BBC, it had to deal with some fairly idiotic people in the Ministry of Information. For instance, a member of the ministry's Empire Division complained once that the Hindustani service had quoted from an editorial in the *Daily Express* which, commenting on a speech by the Secretary of State for India, Leo Amery, said: 'Dominion status has been promised to India before. Mr. Amery is a man who keeps his promises.' The complaint was:'The implication that previous British statesmen have failed to keep their promises is all too obvious.' Quite so, but the BBC was able to tell the ministry coldly that the India Office had approved the use of the quotation.

Japanese broadcasts to India were probably more effective than those from London; in 1943, for example, Bombay was partially evacuated because of threats from the Japanese radio. Britain's response to these transmissions was virtually non-existent.

From early in 1941, the government had wanted the BBC to start a Japanese service; a senior official at the Ministry of Information actually argued that it would keep Japan out of the war, which suggests a credulous faith in the power of radio.

Later, when Japan had occupied most of Britain's colonial possessions in the Far East, the object was to influence official opinion in Tokyo.

The BBC demurred. Short-wave sets were illegal in Japan, except for a handful of senior government officials, so what was the point? It is precisely those officials we want to influence, said the Foreign Office. The Corporation reluctantly agreed but then found great difficulty in recruiting Japanese nationals willing to broadcast. Eventually they found them in the United States, and transmissions began in July 1943.

Soon after the end of the war a senior BBC official visited Japan and reported: 'There seems reason for supposing that our broadcasts were listened to by the Japanese army in the field...In Japan itself, however, it is quite clear that during the war we had few, if indeed any, listeners. Government officials who were in a position to listen to us did not do so.' The service continued after the war and acquired new listeners, but the audience was never large and in 1991 it closed.

CHAPTER SEVEN

Post-War Blues

THE BBC External Services (as they were now to be called) had established their reputation in six years of war. Did they have a continuing role to play in the post-war world? There were cuts in some of the services to Europe even before the end of the war, as countries were liberated. But the Labour government accepted a recommendation by a committee established by its predecessor that Britain should continue to broadcast to the world. In a White Paper in 1946 it explained why:

'The European service retains a large audience... and friends of this country are anxious that it should continue. Moreover, there are clear indications at present that other powers intend to continue to use the broadcast media to put their point of view before the European audience and we cannot afford to let the British viewpoint go by default.'

The White Paper put the External Services on a regular footing after their rapid and haphazard growth during the war. It also laid down principles which remain valid to this day: 'The government intend that the Corporation should remain independent in the preparation of programmes for overseas audiences, although it should obtain from the government departments concerned such information about conditions in those countries and the policy of His Majesty's government towards them as will permit it to plan its programmes in the national interest.' It is the national interest which is invoked, not the interest of the government of the day; the two are not necessarily synonymous.

The Lord President of the Council, Herbert Morrison, explained the government's thinking when he spoke in the debate in the Commons on the White Paper. 'The Corporation,' he said, 'will accept the guidance of the Foreign Office on the nature and scope of its foreign language services, and there will be a very close liaison between the two of them...But once the general character and scope of a service has been laid down the BBC will have complete discretion as to the content of the programmes. This compromise may result in some regrettable incidents if there is a temporary failure of contact between the Foreign Office and the Corporation, but, unless such incidents are to be much more numerous than we expect, they will, I think be a small price to pay for letting the responsibility for broadcasting programmes lie with those best qualified to exercise it.' What this meant (and still means) is that the government decides the languages in which the BBC broadcasts and for how long, pays for them, but does not have control over the result.

The Director-General of the BBC, William Haley, laid down the principles and purpose of the External Services in a document issued in the light of the White Paper. It has to a certain extent been overtaken by a new statement of purpose issued in 1984 (see the final chapter), whose message is much the same, but it is of fundamental importance to the working of the World Service in the post-war years.

The first aim, he said, is to provide 'an accurate, impartial and dispassionate flow of news.' Although it would be seen through British eyes, it should be world-wide in scope, maintain a proper international balance in compilation and selection and be as objective as possible. The greatest importance must be attached to comprehensiveness as well as accuracy. He went on: 'The desire to distort information is in this country rarely in evidence' (this was in 1946).

It was not, he said, the function of the External Services to interfere in the domestic affairs of any other nation. They did not exist in order to throw out governments or change regimes. On matters of international controversy the official British view should be given due prominence, opposing foreign views should be carefully explained and conflicting opinions with serious backing in Britain itself should be given weight, as far as possible according to the strength of that backing.

This last requirement has not always endeared the BBC to the government, notably at the time of Suez.

The definition of serious backing applied to opposing views can also create problems.

BROADCASTING POLICY

Presented by the Lord President of the Council and the Postmaster General to Parliament by Command of His Majesty
July, 1946

LONDON
HIS MAJESTY'S STATIONERY OFFICE
SIXPENCE NET

Cmd. 6852

CONTENTS

The principles governing British broadcasting were set out in this White Paper of July, 1946.

"Do you realise if the Russians do stop jamming the BBC, we'll have a potential audience of 117 million— all squares?"

It was not only an alternative version of the news that Russians had to fear by lifting their jamming; they would also be exposed to western pop music. This is an Evening Standard *cartoon from December, 1959.*

There are those who complain that minority views are not sufficiently reflected in World Service output. How big does a minority have to be before it can be described as having serious backing?

The year of the White Paper also saw the start of broadcasting in Russian. When Hitler invaded the Soviet Union in June 1941 Churchill's speech promising full co-operation was translated into Russian by a member of the BBC staff and broadcast.

But that was the end of it. The Soviet government said a regular service in Russian would serve no useful purpose because all private sets which could receive it had been impounded.

After the war the BBC was told that this restriction had gone, and the Russian service opened on 24 March 1946.

One of its main aims was to express the friendliness of the British people towards the Soviet Union; the Cold War was still in its infancy, although attacks on British policies had already started appearing in the Soviet media. An internal report on the service about a year after it had begun was critical:

'While it is extremely successful in projecting British people at work and at play I do not think it is really using its opportunity to familiarise the Soviet audience with the ideals of tolerance and individual freedom.' The report noted that only the communist *Daily Worker* was quoted in British press comments on a possible revision of the Polish frontier.

After the communist coup in Czechoslovakia in 1948 the tone seems to have changed. An internal report in that year said: 'The subject matter has become less unbalanced in the sense that they no longer preserve so great a detachment from the real and therefore controversial issues of the day'.

The report praised the work of the commentator Anatol Goldberg who it said, 'succeeded astonishingly well in creating an informal and friendly atmosphere, the note being struck being one of regret at the estrangement between Russia and the West. Goldberg himself never criticised Russian methods or motives, and he never argued the Anglo-American case, though occasionally he defined quite clearly the attitude taken up by the Western powers on a particular issue.'

Anatol Goldberg, a Russian who had begun his BBC career in the Monitoring Service, monitoring Spanish broadcasts, remained an outstanding commentator in the Russian service for many years.

He was one of a number of people in Bush House unknown in Britain but with a large following abroad.

A former managing director of External Broadcasting (and author of its history) Gerard Mansell, once told the story of a mother and daughter in Leningrad one of whose favourite games was to elect their own make-believe world government. It included not only world statesmen but also Goldberg, known to them familiarly as Anatoli Maksimovich.

The restrained tone struck by Goldberg and the Russian service as a whole was in contrast to that of the Americans who saw their broadcasts to the Soviet Union as part of an international campaign for freedom and were consequently more polemical. Nor was it universally popular. The service was attacked in the columns of the weekly *Spectator* in 1957 for 'trimming its sails' and 'moral compromise and appeasement'. Later the dissident writer Alexander Solzhenitsyn expressed similar views. BBC broadcasts, he argued, were no better than 'water trickling through your fingers.' It is worth noting, though, that when Solzhenitsyin was

Anatol Goldberg, for many years the BBC's chief commentator on Soviet and Eastern European affairs.

expelled to the West and journalists from all over the world were trying to see him he gave his first interview to a member of the BBC Russian service whose voice he recognised.

Certainly the Soviet authorities did not think they were being appeased. They began jamming the service in 1949, and continued jamming on and off until 1987. They attacked the BBC in violent terms – 'mad agitators and disruptionists', for example, and more picturesquely 'a crying radio crocodile.' It is only in recent years that attacks of this sort have come to an end.

Although a new service had been started, the late forties and early fifties were the worst of times for the External Services. Government, having willed the ends, did not will the means and refused to increase the grant-in-aid in spite of inflation. In 1951, with the outbreak of the Korean war, government spending was severely cut, and the grant-in-aid was reduced.

Services to Latin America were slashed, the General Overseas Service in English reduced, most breakfast and lunchtime transmission to Western Europe and all services to Belgium and Luxembourg brought to an end. Capital expenditure was deferred, although there was an increasing need for new transmitters.

Severe cuts of this nature led Major-General Sir Ian Jacob, then Director of External Broadcasting (and later to become Director-General) to complain bitterly to the Cabinet Office: 'Broadcasting is not something that can be turned on and off like a tap. The audience and the reputation for truth and quality is built up slowly and laboriously. Once sacrificed it is very hard to restore.' Sir Ian Jacob was a former assistant military secretary to the Cabinet, but here he was stating a classical BBC argument which has been repeated again and again.

In opposition the Conservatives had strongly criticised the cuts, but when they took over government in 1951 they froze the grant-in-aid at its reduced level. However, in the face of strong criticism in Parliament and the press the government set up a small committee under Lord Drogheda which came to the conclusion that the drastic cuts in the Latin American service had been a grave mistake, that the General Overseas Service should be restored to 24 hours a day and that more overseas relay stations should be built because of the increased crowding of the short wave bands. But other services should be cut, notably those to Western Europe.

Since those days there have been several more committees which have made recommendations about the External Services. They have mostly been rejected by the BBC or the government on the grounds that they have failed to understand fully its role.

One of the favourite themes has been that the BBC should concentrate on broadcasting in English which, it is argued, is understood by the people who matter, the opinion formers in each country. The BBC has always disputed this, arguing that it is demonstrably untrue and that, anyway, broadcasting is for everyone and cannot be confined to an elite; that would be narrowcasting. In fact, the audience for the vernacular services is far greater than that for the services in English.

Since the fifties there have been new cuts in services, threatened or actual. The reaction of the BBC has sometimes suggested that, unless it holds on to everything it has, Britain's standing in the world will be fatally compromised. But the dire consequences sometimes forecast have not materialised. There has been no discernible change in attitudes towards Britain in, for example, the Scandinavian countries or Italy or Israel, to take a few at random, just because transmissions directed there have come to an end. And, although many language services have been abolished or reduced, others have been created.

The problem has been that cuts were

made for the wrong reasons. They were not because the services were regarded as no longer desirable but because at times of financial crisis all government spending had to be reduced, and the doctrine of 'equality of misery' applied. Long-term interests were ignored.

Perhaps the most damaging cuts were those in planned capital expenditure; relay stations were urgently needed if only to keep up with the competition.

The BBC and the government experienced their most serious disagreement over the Suez crisis of 1956. The issue was simple. The government decided that, together with France and Israel, it would take military action against Egypt to punish President Nasser for nationalising the Suez Canal.

At the time it was described as an Anglo-French 'police action' to keep the armies of Israel and Egypt apart, but it has since become clear that there was collusion with Israel.

There was strong and vocal opposition both at home and abroad. The BBC took the view that it had no choice but to reflect this opposition in the External Services, including transmissions in Arabic and English.

It did two things in particular which upset the government. In its usual review of the British press it quoted a hard-hitting editorial in the Manchester Guardian (as it was then) which described the government's actions as 'an act of folly without justification in any terms but brief expediency.' It also broadcast an attack on the government by the Leader of the Opposition, Hugh Gaitskell, who was exercising his right of reply to Eden's ministerial broadcast. One of the government's complaints was that this was heard by troops waiting at sea to attack Egypt and could affect their morale.

Those were the facts; the fallout was considerable. At one point Eden was said to be so furious that he wanted to take over the BBC. The Foreign Office posted a 'liaison officer' in Bush House, supposedly to supplement the normal channels of communication; his role was never quite clear, and when the crisis was over he went. The government took over a British-owned commercial broadcasting outfit, Sharq al Adna, which transmitted to an Arab audience on medium wave from Cyprus. It used it to broadcast the 'Voice of Britain', anti-Nasser propaganda which seems to have had little effect.

The BBC came under heavy criticism from a group of Conservative MPs in a debate in the Commons after the ceasefire. Various allegations of biased reporting were made, but, as sometimes happens with allegations made with the protection of Parliamentary privilege, they were found to be untrue, and based on hearsay. Sir Ian Jacob, now Director-General, wrote in the staff newspaper Ariel the following January that it was most satisfactory that the careful investigation undertaken by the governors into all the allegations showed that they could not be sustained. He also dealt with the argument that the national interest would have been better served by failing to report the opposition, particularly when the use of force had been decided on:

'Our External Services are world-wide in scope and are heard almost everywhere. They are set by the listener alongside what he hears on his own radio and reads in his own papers....If the BBC is found for the first time to be suppressing significant items of news its reputation would rapidly vanish, and the harm to the national interest done in that event would enormously outweigh any damage caused by displaying to the world the workings of a free democracy.'

The World Service regards Suez as a sort of battle honour and it is the example which is quoted whenever accusations are made that it does what the government orders. Sir Ian Jacob himself said many years later (in a conversation with the author in 1980) that

he thought Eden's threat to take it over was an aberration; he soon realised it couldn't be done. Sir Ian also said that there were no serious repercussions for the BBC from the Suez crisis – Eden resigned after the ceasefire and government policies altered – 'but, of course, ministers don't like us as a rule... the BBC is generally speaking an annoying sore in the flesh, and of course they take it out on the overseas services because they feel very strongly that they should be spouting their policy only.'

Suez coincided with, and to some extent overshadowed, the Hungarian revolution, which was crushed by the Soviet army. On the day before the tanks moved in Budapest Radio broadcast a message of thanks to the BBC for its 'objective information about the people's struggle'. The opinion of a group of Hungarian refugees interviewed in Austria was clear: 'The thing was that the BBC told the truth always. They never promised the impossible. They were never afraid either of saying what was unpleasant. That is why we trusted them.'

The BBC was not the most popular Western broadcaster in Hungary. Both Radio Free Europe and the Voice of America broadcast for longer each day and had more listeners. But a survey among the refugees showed that a large majority (90%) considered the BBC to be the most reliable. And one of the American broadcasting organisations was so struck by this that it sent a team to Bush House to study its methods. It concluded that the reason for the BBC's credibility was that it did not hesitate to include items critical of Britain. So the order went out for a 'credibility item'- something detrimental about the United States – in every bulletin.

By the late fifties all the External Services were finally together in Bush House, originally the home of the European Services only. During and immediately after the war staff had operated from various different

locations, some in the provinces, some in various buildings in London, including a department store in Oxford Street. Now they were all under one roof, although in different wings in the building and sharing it with other occupants, including the Inland Revenue.

After Suez the hours of the Arabic service were increased and the BBC began broadcasting in three African languages, Hausa (for West Africa), Swahili (for East Africa) and Somali. The aim was to counteract broadcasts from Cairo to what were still mostly British colonies; transmissions in Afrikaans were dropped.

It was the prelude to a fundamental shift in attitudes and priorities which was to be a mark of the sixties.

This was the decade when the British Empire was finally brought to an end, with colonies in Africa and the Caribbean in particular being given independence. Africa became increasingly important to the External Services. Its African service, in English and the other three languages, spoke to the newly independent countries, interviewed their leaders and by encompassing the whole continent could be seen as a unifying force. The radio services of many of these countries had been set up with the help of seconded BBC people and their staffs trained by the BBC, so the links remained close. Events in Africa, too, were important enough to be reflected in the general output (although listeners in other parts of the world sometimes complained that there was too much about Africa).

As Empire became Commonwealth the world-wide audience for the BBC was changing. The General Overseas Service

Budapest, 1956. The revolt by Hungarians against their Soviet rulers caused many casualties. The protesters in this truck are picking up the wounded; the Red Cross in the flag is painted with their blood.

Another radio revolution started in the 1950s with the introduction of the transistor. This is the British-made 'Coronet'. 'A British firm has produced a pocket radio for nine and a half guineas – the cheapest yet.'

adventure. In Bush House the scripted talk began to give way to informal, unscripted discussion as a way of exploring current affairs.

With increasing attention being given to the Third World, programmes dealt with issues of particular interest to them, such as economic and social development.

The audience for these programmes grew enormously, thanks to the invention of the transistor. This tiny device, which dates from the fifties, revolutionised radio listening. Until it came into general use nearly all the radio sets in the world were in Europe or North America. But in 20 or so years after 1956 the number in Africa south of the Sahara grew from under half a million to over 22 million. In China it went from one million to about 50 million, in India from one to 18 million. A large proportion could receive short-wave transmissions; in many cases their own national radio was on short-wave.

As audiences grew and programmes changed there was also a change in the perception of the World Service, on the part of the government and the public in general. For a period during the seventies there was a succession of cuts as government expenditure was trimmed.

None was enormous in itself, but what was described as 'death by a thousand cuts' had the effect of reducing services for comparatively small savings. In 1979, in the first year of the new Conservative government, came a demand for savings of four million pounds, ten per cent of operating costs. No fewer than seven services were under threat. In the end some were saved, if reduced, and only the Italian, Spanish and Maltese services disappeared. Because of the publicity surrounding this episode many people to this day vaguely associate the World Service with being under threat from the government.

But with the cuts (in 1981) came the

became the World Service in 1965, but perhaps more striking as a symbol of change was the re-naming of the short bulletin of British news which sometimes followed the world news. From Home *News from Britain* it became *News About Britain*. The stereotype of the average listener was no longer the British expatriate – perhaps a planter sitting on his verandah listening to London with a sundowner in his hand, probably an inaccurate picture but an evocative one. The stereotype now is an upwardly mobile Asian male with a bicycle. Expatriates form a very small proportion of listeners.

To cater for this new audience the BBC devised new types of programme. The sixties were in any case a time of great change in Britain, and the output reflected this. Sir Hugh Greene became Director-General of the BBC in 1960 and ushered in a time of greater experimentation and

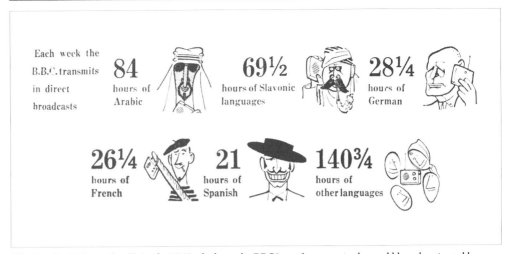

The Sunday Telegraph *of March, 1962, deplores the BBC's performance in the world broadcasting tables.*

beginning of a ten-year programme to increase audibility (discussed in detail later). In 1991 the World Service came out with an increase of six per cent in real terms to improve programmes – the first time government money had been given for that purpose. And it was broadcasting for more than 800 hours a week, the highest level since the war. Several factors contributed to this positive outcome, and some of them are described in the following chapters. It is time to look a little behind the scenes...

CHAPTER EIGHT

Getting the Message Over

INTERNATIONAL broadcasting began with short waves and will continue on short waves to many parts of the world, in spite of the problems associated with them. Short waves, reflected by the ionosphere, can transmit to faraway places, unaffected by earthbound barriers such as buildings and mountains. They are also known as High Frequency (HF) – explanations are in order for the non-technical.

If you imagine radio waves as being a greatly enlarged and speeded-up version of the waves you make by dropping a stone in a pond, the wavelength is the distance in metres between their crests. The number of crests passing a given point in one second is the frequency, expressed as multiples of Hertz, named after Heinrich Hertz, who in the late 19th century verified the existence of these electro-magnetic waves.

Radio waves travel at the speed of light – 300 million metres a second. So with a wavelength of 30 metres, for example, the number of crests passing a fixed point each second will be ten million – ten Megahertz. This gives a mathematical formula for conversion. Divide either metres or Megahertz into 300, and the result is given in terms of the other.

For example, to find the wavelength (distance from crest to crest) of 15.07 Mhz, divide 300 by 15.07. This gives 19.91 metres. Alternatively, given a wavelength of 31.88 metres, divide 300 by 31.88, which gives 9.412 Mhz.

There are inherent difficulties with short waves. Their properties were first explored by amateur radio enthusiasts in the nineteen-twenties, but their efforts were hit-and-miss because little was known about the behaviour of the ionosphere and the way it is affected by the sun:.'A frequency that gave satisfactory transmission over a particular path in summer might be useless in winter and one that was satisfactory in summer one year might be useless at the same season next year. It naturally took a long time to work out a system of prediction that would enable the optimum frequency to be chosen for any path at any time of day and at a particular point in the sunspot cycle...It was not until 1962 that an ionospheric sounder carried by a satellite was able to give information about the properties of the upper part of the ionosphere.' (*BBC Engineering 1922-1972* Edward Pawley, BBC Publications 1972)

There are other constraints. Only a

limited range can be used; those that are too short pass right through the ionosphere and are lost in space, those that are too long are absorbed. The sun causes atmospheric disturbances from time to time, and these affect reception. An ionospheric storm, which can go on for several days, brings about a fading of the higher frequencies; a sudden ionospheric disturbance seldom lasts more than an hour but affects transmissions in lower frequencies during daylight. In addition to all this the signal becomes weaker each time it is reflected back from earth.

One problem which has become far less acute is that of jamming. A great deal of ingenuity had to be used in order to overcome jamming of broadcasts to the Soviet bloc, but this has ended (at the time of writing, that is; who knows what may happen in the future?) Jamming has a long history. The Nazis jammed the Soviet radio in the nineteen-thirties, for example, the French jammed German broadcasts at the

beginning of the Second World War. The British never went in for it, arguing that it was more trouble than it was worth because whatever you did the facts would emerge anyway; it was seen as the sign of a guilty conscience. The Russians began jamming the BBC in 1949 and continued on and off (during periods of détente) until 1987. The Chinese took to it after the massacre in Tianenmen Square in 1989, and the Iraqis tried to jam the BBC Arabic service during the Gulf war.

Jamming takes two main forms. One is simply a continuous noise, rather like electrical interference, which drowns out the signal on a given frequency. The other, known as a programme jammer, takes the form of continuous speech or music which sounds like ordinary interference. The Soviet Union spent vast sums on this activity; now transmitters formerly used for jamming are available to broadcast programmes.

One of the main problems for short wave broadcasters to-day is congestion. As more and more countries decided to set up their own broadcasting systems, including external broadcasting, the short-wave bands became more and more crowded. The result is that trawling through the short-wave bands is rather like taking a day trip to the Tower of Babel, with various whistling and crackling sounds thrown in. There must, you would think, be a better way.

There are, in fact, several, although they do not provide a complete answer. One is to send recorded programmes abroad, to be broadcast by other countries on their own networks. This actually began at the same time as the Empire Service itself, in 1932. Discs were shipped out to stations in the Empire. Their sound quality was better than programmes transmitted direct, they could be broadcast at times convenient to the local radio and repeated if necessary, and they could be heard by people who did not own short wave receivers.

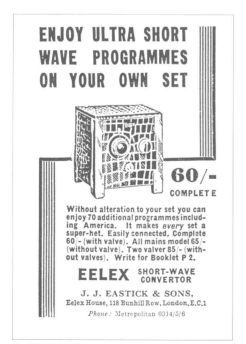

In 1933, for three pounds, you could convert your wireless set to enable it to receive ultra-short wave.

The BBC was full of earnest endeavour in those days, and the stated intention of these programmes was to project 'the life, art and industry of the mother country' to those who still regarded it as home. Among the discs was a medley of old English songs, a musical comedy especially written for broadcasting and *Children's Hour*. A small charge was made to cover the cost of securing the broadcasting rights, but in 1939 it was noted that American firms and the Nazis were providing recorded programmes either free of charge or at a very low cost.

This meant that broadcasters in the countries of the Empire were using plenty of non-British, even anti-British, material.

The Foreign Office was now sufficiently alarmed to set up its own Joint Broadcasting Council to provide recorded programmes for abroad, to extend awareness of Britain and its way of life. In 1941 this was merged with the BBC operation to form the London Transcription Service which was subsidised by the government. In 1949, still subsidised, it became the BBC Transcription Service.

The subsidy has been cut, and the BBC has to compete with a large number of radio stations which supply recorded material free. All the same, it does a thriving business in supplying discs and tapes to countries all over the world – plays, concerts, comedy programmes, quizzes and talks. Most have already been broadcast in the domestic services, but some are specially commissioned. It also distributes Topical Tapes, covering such subjects as international politics and economics, development issues, science, books and a programme for the Caribbean.

In spite of the name, it is not possible to be topical in programmes distributed once a week by airmail, however cunningly they are written. Direct broad-casting is essential for news and current affairs and sport, for example. The story of direct broadcasting has not always been a happy one.

At the beginning of the war the only

short-wave transmitters were at Daventry. It was from there that the Empire Service began in 1932, and where many pioneering developments in short wave broadcasting were carried out, including work on operating unattended transmitters. So there was some sadness when it was announced in 1991 that it was finally to close.

The 'triple expansion' of the war saw many new short wave transmitting sites – at Rampisham in Dorset, for example, Start Point in Devon, Clevedon in Somerset, Skelton in what is now Cumbria, and Wooferton in Shropshire, used after the war to relay the Voice of America. New medium-wave transmitters were also installed for Western Europe, and a high power long wave station near Spurn Head came into operation in 1943 to beam a signal into Germany. With four 200 kilowatt transmitters, it was at the time 'the most powerful broadcasting station in the world' (Edward Pawley). It was closed in 1953 for lack of money. It was an impressive effort in difficult conditions, and many of these transmitters continued to give sterling service for many years after the war.

But in the postwar years things began to get difficult. British colonies became independent and stopped re-broadcasting the BBC as a matter of course. The transistor revolution provided a huge potential audience, but one which needed a signal which could be picked up fairly easily by a set which was far simpler than the old high-quality valve sets. And international competition became intense, with the BBC losing its leading position. The Soviet Union overtook it in 1955 in the number of hours broadcast, and China followed in 1960. The Americans (Voice of America, Radio Free Europe and Radio Liberty) and the Egyptians under Nasser also forged ahead during the fifties.

The best programme in the world is worthless if nobody can hear it, and the

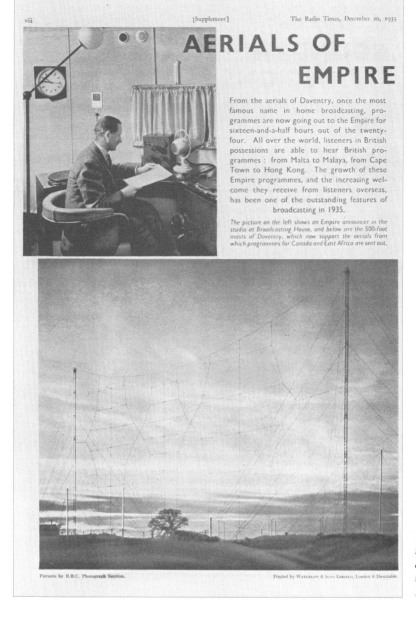

AERIALS OF EMPIRE

From the aerials of Daventry, once the most famous name in home broadcasting, programmes are now going out to the Empire for sixteen-and-a-half hours out of the twenty-four. All over the world, listeners in British possessions are able to hear British programmes : from Malta to Malaya, from Cape Town to Hong Kong. The growth of these Empire programmes, and the increasing welcome they receive from listeners overseas, has been one of the outstanding features of broadcasting in 1935.

The picture on the left shows an Empire announcer in the studio at Broadcasting House, and below are the 500-foot masts of Daventry, which now support the aerials from which programmes for Canada and East Africa are sent out.

Pictures by B.B.C. Photograph Section.   Printed by WATERLOW & SONS LIMITED, London & Dunstable

The BBC Empire short-wave station at Daventry; from the Radio Times *of 20 December, 1935.*

problem of audibility has concerned the BBC for several decades; even now it has not been completely solved. Before the Second World War it was realised that it was essential to have relay stations in various parts of the world able to re-transmit on frequencies suitable for local conditions. The first, at Tebrau in Malaya (as it was then) was not, however, opened until 1949. It has since closed and its operations moved to

Singapore. The cuts in government spending which were a feature of the fifties had their effect on plans for more relay stations. It was agreed by everybody that they were needed – then it was found necessary to defer the capital expenditure.

The transmitter in Cyprus, seized by the government to put over anti-Nasser propaganda at the time of Suez, was handed to the BBC as a relay station when the crisis

In 1949 the BBC built anti-jamming devices at Tatsfield, to override Russian interference on BBC broadcasts.

At the height of the Russian jamming only 12 per cent of western broadcasting was unaffected. The engineer locates the jamming on his cathode-ray tube.

was over. In the sixties a relay was opened on Ascension Island in the middle of the Atlantic Ocean, able to send signals to West Africa and in the opposite direction to Latin America. Later in the decade the Omani island of Masirah was used to boost the medium wave signal to the countries in the Gulf area, and in the early seventies the BBC co-operated with the German broadcasting organisation Deutsche Welle to open a station in Antigua to serve the Caribbean and the American continent.

All this was good as far as it went, but it did not go far enough. Other countries were doing better – more powerful transmitters, more relay stations. There were areas of the world where it was difficult, if not impossible, to hear the BBC. In East Africa, for instance, the German overseas radio Deutsche Welle had more listeners in English and Swahili; it could be heard better from a relay in central Africa.

There were reviews and reports; again everybody agreed that it was necessary to strengthen the signal; again there were delays. But at last the Labour government of James Callaghan agreed to a programme of

improvements costing £100 million, and the Conservative government of Margaret Thatcher began to carry it out in 1981 – at the same time demanding cuts in programmes to pay for it.

The programme took ten years to complete. The first thing was to modernise the transmitters in Britain and dispose of those which had been in operation since the war. The medium wave transmissions to Europe were transferred from Crowborough in Sussex, where signal strength was weakened by having to go partially overland, to Orfordness, by the sea in Suffolk. Powerful new transmitters were installed at some sites – ten 500 kilowatt automatically controlled transmitters at Rampisham, for instance, sending a strong signal to Eastern Europe, the Middle East and America. The transmitter at Skelton, in operation since the war, was finally closed in March 1990 and eighteen months later a new one was opened.

An important part of the programme was the building of a new control room in Bush House itself, formally opened in 1991. Transmitting for 24 hours a day in English and all the other languages is a task of enormous complexity. Programmes originate from over 40 studios and have to be sent to transmitters in Britain and relay stations abroad – about 75 transmitters at 17 different sites. Connecting each studio to the right transmitter, and to incoming signals, is the job of the control room, aided by a MIRA computer.

Abroad, too, there were big improvements – new transmitters in Cyprus and Ascension Island to strengthen the signal and two completely new relay stations, in Hong Kong and Seychelles in the Indian Ocean. The Hong Kong transmitter made an enormous difference to the audience in China. Before it was opened in 1987 listeners in cities such as Shanghai and Peking, a long way from the relay in Singapore, found listening to the BBC difficult; it was sometimes drowned out by rivals, such as Moscow Radio and Voice of America. Both the Hong Kong transmitter and that in Seychelles, which covers East Africa, are able to operate unattended.

There is also a relay in Lesotho, for southern Africa. For many years it concentrated on short waves, but it is now able to put out a medium wave signal, more appropriate for South Africa. There is an FM transmitter in Berlin and reciprocal arrangements in the use of certain transmitters with other international broadcasters such as Voice of America.

From 1982 onwards the BBC took advantage of satellite broadcasting to send signals by satellite to its relay stations. It used two Intelsat V geostationary satellites, one over the Indian Ocean, the other over the Atlantic. In some cases it built its own earth stations. On Ascension Island the receiving dish had to be sited below ground to shield it from interference from the existing transmissions. Using satellites and so avoiding the vagaries of the ionosphere has meant improved reception; the signals arrive in 'studio quality'.

Satellites have another use; other broadcasters can take the transmissions and put them out themselves. This is now happening on a fairly large scale, and is another way of overcoming the disadvantages of short wave. In any case in many countries, such as in Western Europe, short wave

listening is rapidly declining. Improvements in sound reproduction mean that people are no longer prepared to accept poor quality on the radio – unless it is their hobby. Frequency Modulation (FM) otherwise known as Very High Frequency (VHF) gives much better reception and is now standard in advanced countries. But its geographical range is small; it is impossible to broadcast to the world on FM from Britain. So the World Service found another way.

In the last few years there has been a large increase in the number of local, often commercial, FM stations in the developed world. Their newsgathering resources are usually small, and many of them are glad to relay the BBC. Agreement was reached in 1986 for the American Public Radio network to take World Service news and current affairs programmes off the Atlantic satellite and distribute it to its affiliated stations. Later the agreement was extended to include any programme. In 1987 the BBC gained access to a satellite covering most of Europe. Now it is being heard on FM in English or

"WHO WON? RADIO MOSCOW OR THE B.B.C.?"

In 1955 jamming was still going on: not even football was spared...

the language of the country where it is re-broadcast. France, Finland, Greece and Germany are among them, and there are likely to be more. The Latin American Service in Spanish and Portuguese is now available via PanAmSat-1 and is being re-broadcast in more than half a dozen countries. Some fifty stations in Australia and New Zealand relay programmes.

Of course, the English service has been re-broadcast in English-speaking countries from the earliest days. Although most of the larger countries of the Commonwealth decided to drop the BBC when they became independent, smaller ones, notably in the Caribbean and the Pacific, still put out World Service news and news-related programmes at certain times of day.

The latest developments are different; they can cover the whole range of programmes, they are heard in excellent quality on local stations, and many are in foreign languages. Some are paid for; it depends what the market will bear.

But local re-broadcasting is not seen as the complete answer to the problems of short waves. For one thing, it pre-supposes a sophisticated communications system which many countries do not possess yet. It removes control from the BBC and puts it in the hands of the re-broadcaster, and it can be stopped at any time, for commercial or political reasons. For much of the world, short waves are still the answer.

But there are still black spots such as northern India, where listening is difficult. Since the Hindi service has the largest audience of any of them – including the English service – this is obviously not a satisfactory situation. The BBC plans to build a relay in Thailand to remedy it. Latin America and parts of the former Soviet Union are also target areas. The fact is that the ten-year audibility programme has simply brought the World Service up to the level of its competitors – and they are planning further developments: Voice of America alone announced some years ago a massive programme of more than a hundred 500-kilowatt installations.

In the words of Dennis Thompson, Head of Broadcast Coverage Department: 'We were behind many of our major competitors, and we've redressed the balance to a certain extent. But it's like running up a down escalator.'

CHAPTER NINE

Listening to the World: the Monitoring Services

EARLY IN 1991, television teams from various countries made their way to a large country house to the west of London. They were filming the activities of the only comprehensive source of information about what was going on inside Iraq during the Gulf War; – the BBC Monitoring service. It formed part of many television, radio and newspaper features at the time; there were 36 journalistic visits altogether, not including the continuous presence of BBC radio and television.

The visitors came from Japan, Canada, the United States and other countries. At one time a Dutch TV crew was filming a BBC TV crew as it was doing a live interview into a bulletin. At another, two TV crews were filming the activities of a radio reporter and a Japanese crew were filming them doing so. The BBC Monitoring service was not only reporting the news; it was itself making the news all over the world.

It has not always been so. In its early days its existence was hardly known to the public. Monitoring in the BBC sense of the word means listening to the radio (and now watching television) of other countries and reporting what it says. It began in a small way in the thirties, when it was thought it might be

useful to listen to Axis broadcasts and reply to them direct. Shorthand-typists diligently transcribed their notes of the violent propaganda that was a feature of the transmissions from Fascist Italy and Nazi Germany. It was decided that it was not for the BBC to indulge in a sort of slanging match or rebuttal of what was alleged in these broadcasts.

But when war became imminent it became important to know what the enemy was saying. In 1939 the Ministry of Information asked the BBC to set up a monitoring operation and agreed to pay for it. The service was established in August, at first in Wood Norton, near Evesham in Worcestershire; like many BBC departments at the time it was sent away from London to avoid air raids. At first the emphasis was on listening to German broadcasts, but as the war widened it became necessary to hear others as well. At the beginning of 1940, after the Soviet Union had attacked Finland, Scandinavian monitors were recruited; one day a blonde girl wearing white boots was observed coming down the stairs at the house where some of the monitors lived. 'Are you Finnish?' she was asked. 'She looked completely terrified, replied: 'No, I'm just beginning' and made off rapidly in the direction of the typing pool. She was a new typist. (taken from *Assigned to Listen*, by Olive Renier and Vladimir Rubinstein, BBC, 1986)

In 1943 the Monitoring service moved to its present site, Caversham Park, just outside Reading. The reason for the move was that the government was afraid that the Germans were developing an atomic bomb. This would make London uninhabitable, and secret contingency plans were made to move the whole BBC to Wood Norton.

The Monitoring service had grown so much that there would be no room unless it left. For security reasons the move could not be explained, and the staff were unhappy about what they considered to be the insensitive way the change was carried out. They were concerned about finding somewhere to live in Caversham, for example, and offended by the attitude of Ogilvie, the Director-General, that, whatever their worries, they had to obey orders. Three senior members of the Monitoring Service resigned in protest to join the forces. The ill-feeling engendered by this episode was one of the factors that led the BBC governors to retire Ogilvie. Caversham Park is actually a very pleasant environment, with extensive grounds and graceful vistas over the Thames valley. The building dates from the 19th century, the home of a Welsh ironmaster, and it has recently been enlarged by the BBC.

Most of the wartime monitors were foreigners living in Britain. They were talented people and some became well-known after the war – George Weidenfeld, the publisher, for instance, and Geoffrey Grigson, the poet. Monitoring quickly became a 24 hour a day, seven days a week occupation, and most of the services which it offers to-day had their beginnings during the war. It provided news to government departments as well as the BBC; verbatim texts of speeches by the Nazi leaders were

In studio 18, in 1949, four commentators prepare to start their half-hour battle with the Russian jamming-stations.

Caversham Park was a somewhat decrepit stately home when first acquired by the BBC, but is now extended and refurbished.

particularly useful. The service departments were interested in lists of prisoners of war; the German service, as noted earlier, received in advance the text of Goebbel's weekly commentaries, and a daily digest of world broadcasts was instituted.

In June1944, on D-Day, the Monitoring service received the news of the landings in Normandy from the German radio before the allies had announced it themselves – and the BBC broadcast the news. Later in 1944 it heard Hitler announce on the radio that he had survived the bomb plot against him. In May the following year, to the strains of Bruckner, the North German Home Service announced: 'Our Fuehrer Adolf Hitler, fighting for his last breath against Bolshevism, fell for Germany this afternoon.'

During the war the United States set up its own monitoring service, known as the

Foreign Broadcasting Information Service (FBIS). The two organisations co-operated from the early days – the first Americans arrived in Wood Norton in 1942 – and in 1948 this co-operation was confirmed in a formal agreement. The BBC and FBIS effectively divide the world up between them. The BBC covers Europe, including the Soviet Union as far as Afghanistan, Iran, parts of the Middle East, the Mediterranean and East Africa; it has a unit in Kenya. The Americans cover the rest of the world. There is a certain amount of overlapping. It is an arrangement that is said to work well; a 'shining example in terms of international co-operation of how well it can be done' is one description. Certainly it gives the two countries access to a great deal of material which would be far more expensive to collect if each tried to cover the whole world itself.

The receiving aerials are at Crowsley Park, a few miles away, and there are satellite dishes in the grounds of Caversham Park itself; some radio transmissions, as well as television, now go by satellite. In the listening room the monitors sit with headphones, making notes as they listen. The transmissions are recorded, and when they make translations they work from the recordings.

The wartime generation has gone, and many monitors now are British graduates. Many, too, are skilled in more than one language, so they can be switched from one to another as the need arises. Monitors have been described by a former member of the service as being sedentary press correspondents. They gather their news by sitting and listening, and often they gather it before anyone else.

Their job is not as easy as it may sound. Ramon Silva, a member of the service from 1939 to 1972, pointed out in a *Monitoring* booklet published in 1979 that, apart from good hearing, a monitor needed 'a wide

knowledge of current affairs, politics, economics, history, world geography; a knowledge in depth of the language or languages being monitored, and a fluent and idiomatic command of English.' Accuracy and speed were the keynotes, he said, and he went on: 'The monitor wages a constant struggle against the unreliability of sound. In that struggle, background knowledge and an intuitive gift for mental association are the major allies.'

The use of satellites for radio transmissions has in some cases made them easier to hear, and a good deal of material comes in written form from foreign news agencies. But there are still pitfalls. Mishearing can lead to mistranslation; that is why a recording is available for checking and re-checking. Sometimes even if the words are clear the meaning may be obscure or ambiguous. Television presents its own problems; a picture lays itself open to subjective interpretations.

Perhaps the most important attribute is experience. It takes three months to train a monitor and up to another two years or so to reach full proficiency. Experience brings what has been described as a sixth sense, an ability to detect possible change by noting the behaviour of a radio station. In 1953 a Russian language monitor heard on the Soviet radio a poem about the approaching death of an ageing eagle. It did not form part of a regular programme and, suspecting it heralded something portentous, he translated it. Soon afterwards the death of Stalin was announced.

Many dramatic announcements have been picked up by the Monitoring service – President Nasser's nationalisation of the Suez Canal, for example, the Soviet crushing of the Hungarian revolution and later of the 'Prague Spring.' It played its own part in ending the Cuban missile crisis in 1962. At an acute and dangerous stage it monitored a Moscow Radio broadcast in which the

Soviet leader, Nikita Khruschev, replying to a message from President Kennedy, said: 'The Soviet government has ordered the dismantling of the bases and the despatch of the equipment to the USSR. I appreciate your assurance that the United States will not invade Cuba.'

The message was flashed to Washington via the FBIS and Kennedy replied immediately, 'although,' he said, ' I have not yet received the official text, because I attach tremendous significance to acting quickly with a view to solving the Cuban crisis.'

The overthrow of President Ceausescu of Romania was foreshadowed at Caversham. Listening to a live relay of a rally he was addressing, the monitor noticed what sounded like a scream; the broadcast stopped, to be resumed later. The recording was played over and over again for checking and finally the BBC correspondent in Central Europe was alerted.

The attempted coup against President Gorbachev in the summer of 1991 was heralded by radio. Just before three o'clock in the morning of 19 August all the separate radio channels merged into one. According to Henry Pavlovich, Editor of News and Publications, breaking the normal pattern in this way often foreshadows a major development, although 'it can just mean someone has cocked it up.' In this case the Russian language monitor immediately notified the news desk, which in turn alerted Bush House. At ten past three TASS, the Soviet news agency, announced the formation of a state emergency committee to run the country because (it said) of Mr Gorbachev's state of health.

Monitors put their material into a computer which distributes it to customers. One is the newsroom, where it is edited to form part of its newsfile. It is also sent to news organisations, including the BBC, and government departments, such as the FCO. It is in effect a news agency, with the important difference from others that it does not make any comment or 'gloss' on the news but simply reports what is said. Other copies go to editors who prepare a daily Summary of World Broadcasts which is sent to three thousand subscribers. This comes in separate sections dealing with different geographical areas – the USSR; Eastern Europe; the Far East; and the Middle East, Africa and Latin America; there is a weekly economic report for each area.

The Monitoring service also produces a regular bulletin of information about worldwide developments in broadcasting – the appearance of clandestine stations, for example, or this fascinating item from Volgograd in the Soviet Union in May 1991:

'A peal of bells sounded out to-day as the signature of the birth of the new commercial radio station "Vedo". It has been possible for it to go on the air thanks to a former 'jammer', the equipment of which was idle once the ban on alien voices was lifted.' The announcement, from the Soviet news agency TASS, explained that some of the programmes would come from the Voice of America and the German station, Deutsche Welle, and other foreign broadcasters. But most of the time would be given to 'the problems of small businesses and lessons in economics and marketing.'

The Monitoring service itself is becoming increasingly aware of the importance of marketing. It sells its publications, in particular the Summary of World Broadcasts to a wide variety of customers, at least half of them overseas. They include journalists, researchers, libraries and commercial firms with a particular interest in, for example, developments in Eastern Europe. Increasingly the material goes not as printed copy but via computer. It is already sold to three different databases, one in the United States. During the Gulf War the service sold a special service to newspapers at a flat rate of £100 a day. In 1992 it will be publishing

Known to its inhabitants as 'Babel Town', monitors listen to broadcasts from all over the world.

its first *Glossary of World Affairs* in association with Longmans, the publishers.

The BBC in general is nowadays expected to earn money to offset the licence fee. The Monitoring Service is separately funded by a grant-in-aid from the Foreign Office, but it, too, is required to double its money from selling its products over the next few years. (Gross receipts 1990/91 were three-quarters of a million pounds.)

At the same time it has received a 14% increase in its grant for the three years until 1994. This is to pay for a big expansion in its services. The changes in the Soviet Union and Eastern Europe have meant that many more radio stations have opened up there and, unlike the old days, they are no longer all following the same line. The end of communism and the formation of a Commonwealth of Independent States has resulted in a variety of views and discussion of such social problems as alcoholism and

drug abuse which were never mentioned before the days of glasnost.

To cope with this information explosion more staff are being recruited and new languages monitored. The regular number of languages monitored is 30, sometimes rising to nearly 40 (the Americans monitor others, bringing the total to nearly 80, from 130 countries). The new ones are from Central Asia; Turkmen, Khazak, Uzbek, for instance. This is a long way from Caversham, but they can be heard through a remote-controlled receiver, based closer to the area and sending the broadcasts over a telephone line.

The Gulf War put the Monitoring service under strain. The output doubled; staff had give up their days off to work extra shifts. Several of them spent some time catering for the needs of the visiting journalists. One problem was the proliferation of radio stations, including the 'Mother of Battles' radio, the 'Voice of Free Iraq', 'Holy Mecca',

'Voice of Peace' and 'Voice of the Gulf'.

At the same time, developments in the Baltic states and Somalia, although overshadowed by the Gulf war coverage by most of the world's media, still had to be watched. The monitoring service was consequently first with the news of the overthrow of President Siad Barre.

The Gulf war itself provided some 'scoops' – the reported killing of an allied prisoner of war in an air raid, for example, and Iraq's rupture of diplomatic relations with the countries of the allied coalition. The work of the service was praised. There was a message of appreciation from 'very senior sources' in the Cabinet Office and a congratulatory Early Day Motion in the Commons.

Accuracy came before 'scoops'. During the war Saddam Hussein made a speech in which he mentioned the word withdrawal for the first time. The American news agency, Associated Press, rushed out a story while Saddam Hussein was still speaking saying he had just agreed to withdraw.

The Monitoring service came under great pressure to confirm the story. It refused to do so because the Iraqi leader had gone on to mention conditions. In the end its stand was justified by the facts.

Thanks to all the publicity it received during the Gulf War the Monitoring service is probably better known now than it has ever been. It has usually been in the background, performing a vital but unsung service. But those who knew about it also knew its value. The FBIS summed it up in a plaque it presented in 1970: 'Presented to the BBC Monitoring service, Steadfast Partner in a Changing World.'

BBC staff monitoring radio transmissions from around the world in the converted drawing-room of Caversham, in 1952.

CHAPTER TEN

News for the World: the Newsroom

BEHIND the measured tones of the news-reader lies a series of complex activities, sometimes carried out at great speed and under great pressure. More than a million words flow into the Bush House newsroom every day. They come from the main international agencies, Reuter, Associated Press (AP), United Press International (UPI), Agence France-Presse (AFP); from the domestic agency, the Press Association (PA); from the Monitoring Service and from BBC reporters and correspondents at home and abroad.

Most of this verbiage is thrown away. Copies go first to two people called copytasters, whose job is to discard what is obviously dross. One works to a central writing unit, the other to the various regional desks serving particular parts of the world. News items are written on the basis of this material for use in bulletins – more than 200 a day – in the 38 languages (including English) in which the BBC broad-casts. At any hour of the night or day there is likely to be a bulletin on or about to be on the air, so the newsroom is at work 24 hours a day, 365 days a year, the staff working in shifts. They number about 120 journalists.

During the war it was difficult to find people with the right qualifications and some oddballs came in, to stay in the postwar years. Among them was a copytaster who, when the first flash announcing Stalin's death came in, chuckled: 'These Russians will say anything' and threw it away (luckily, it was soon retrieved). There was an editor who during an all-night shift was plied with whisky by an English newsreader and at the end of the shift reported him for drinking. Another brought his pet chihuahua to work whenever he did a night shift. One man spent his time running his travel company from the office telephone. And there was a lady known for her sharp tongue who after reading her annual report stormed into the newsroom fuming: 'Which of you bastards said I'd mellowed?'

A new computer system (EDiT) which came into operation in January 1992 – behind schedule because of technical problems -is revolutionising the distribution of news material within Bush House. It has been described as 'probably the largest and most complex system of its kind in the world' (*The Guardian*), with 1,000 terminals, 300 printers and 100 km of fibre-optic cabling. is used not only to make news items and talks and other material available to language services in a number of different languages but also, for the first time, the output of the international news agencies and correspondents' despatches. In the words of Managing Director John Tusa: 'This material will enhance our programme-making and contribute to making the journalism of the World Service a more truly collaborative venture, with departments discussing and exchanging information and ideas.'

Members of language sections are now encouraged to be journalists in their own right, not simply announcer/translators, and this development will clearly help them in that aim. But together with this euphoric vision of the future went a warning. News agencies can mislead and lead to inaccuracies; news stories must not be altered without reference to the newsroom.

From the early days the newsroom was responsible for the content of every bulletin, no matter what language it was in. The journalists in the newsroom are mostly British (or Australasian) and do not necessarily have specialist knowledge of the areas being broadcast to. This has certain advantages; they can take a broader, less parochial, view of the news than might otherwise be the case, and have a healthy scepticism towards 'experts'.

But they may also misjudge the audience. There used to be a good deal of argument with the language services, some of it fierce, over whether or not the most appropriate items had been included in bulletins – a continuation of the 'creative tension' that had flourished during the war.

One example from some years ago: The newsroom wished to include as second headline in a Turkish language bulletin the news that the Pope had relaxed his ban on celebrating the Mass in Latin. Since the population of Turkey is predominantly Muslim, this was of no conceivable interest to them, and the headline was eventually withdrawn after protests.

Arguments of this nature are now reported to have diminished because the language sections prepare their own bulletins, but using only stories provided by the newsroom – a recent change of breathtaking simplicity. It seems to have done more than reduce arguments; it has identified new areas of interest. The Somali service, for example, turned out to be particularly interested in events in the southern republics of the Soviet Union, where there are fellow-Muslims, but not, as one might have expected, in southern Africa.

All this – including the advanced technology – is another stage in the evolution of the newsroom, which has changed enormously since the war. At one time, until some thirty years ago, the operation was divided. There was a Centre Desk on the third floor supplying the main news stories, and regional newsrooms, on different floors adjacent to the language services. For example, there was an East European newsroom on the fifth floor, close to its own clients, a Central European newsroom on the sixth floor, a German on the seventh and so on. Sub-editors would make up individual bulletins for the various services, using their own regional stories and news items from Centre Desk which were run off on a duplicating machine and carried around the building by elderly ladies in carpet slippers or distributed by Lamson tube, a pipe through which documents can be transported by compressed air.

The system allowed for close contacts between the news department and the language services; perhaps it was too close, bearing in mind that the Cold War was at its height and sub-editors might be influenced by some of the Cold War attitudes of the people they dealt with. At any rate, in the interest of efficiency, the separate regional newsrooms came to an end, and all bulletins were produced in a central newsroom.

It might be said that radio did not come fully to the newsroom until 1970. In that year *Radio Newsreel* was dropped from its nightly

spot on the *Light Programme* (now Radio 2) and became a purely overseas programme. Responsibility for producing it passed from Broadcasting House to Bush House. Editors found they were no longer simply preparing a bulletin for somebody else to read but were having to produce a programme of different voiced reports, technically more demanding.

Radio Newsreel has now been laid to rest after 50 years, to be replaced on the English service by *Newsdesk*, a half hour compendium of news, correspondents' reports, and various other delights, such as British news, a review of the British press or a sports bulletin; and, more recently, *Newshour*, a mixture of news and current affairs, once regarded as two

distinct animals in the BBC.

In their working lives journalists do not often discuss what constitutes news; it is taken for granted. It is, though, invariably on the agenda of training courses. The sort of question posed to the students would be something like this: Is news 'a recent event of interest, importance or significance'? If so, to whom? Or is it, as a cynical American description once had it, something somebody wants to conceal? ('all the rest is public relations'). The BBC has at various times tried to pin down the elusive concept of news. In 1926 it was defined as 'what those in control of the BBC think listeners should hear.' This sounds chillingly Stalinist, and

The heart of the BBC European service, the centre desk in Bush House, in 1957.

things have changed since 1926. But of course every bulletin reflects what somebody – the editor – thinks listeners should hear, although now the criteria may be different.

During the seventies the Corporation prepared a study on the broadcasting of news. This went through the various definitions; quoted T.S. Eliot's 'Where is the wisdom we have lost in knowledge? Where is the knowledge we have lost in information?' – an appeal, it would seem, for less news – and concluded: 'The news value of a story is what a journalist recognises when he has been brought up in the editorial tradition of a particular newsroom or office. The BBC tradition is to tell people accurately and

honestly about the most important things going on in the world.'

This still leaves unanswered questions – who decides what are the most important things going on in the world, and on what do they base their decisions? But it does make the point that news varies according to the organisation you work for. What is news for the World Service is unlikely to be news for *The Sun* newspaper and vice-versa. Trained journalists soon learn to distinguish, and a news sense is almost a conditioned reflex. But, as will be argued a little later, what is regarded as 'news' is not necessarily those events which turn out to have been the most important to the course of the world.

The guiding formula for the World Service – world news as seen from London – is a sufficiently broad description to allow for differences in judgement. Indeed, there is a perpetual debate. For example, should every news bulletin be much the same, irrespective of the area to which it is beamed or should concessions be made for regional interests, including countries where the bulletin may be re-broadcast? Like everything else in radio news this largely depends on what is available. There will be no arguments over a major story – the first shots in the Gulf War, for example, or the Moscow coup of August 1991. It is when the story is less obviously important or less relevant to a particular audience that there are problems. During the sixties there was some grumbling over the amount of space devoted to Africa, especially Rhodesia, in bulletins directed to other parts of the world.

In practice, there is usually a standard bulletin with some regional variations , but there can still be an argument over the degree of regionalisation. When the Prime Minister of Barbados, Tom Adams, died in 1985 the news was carried in World Service bulletins for hours – then dropped for the bulletin re-broadcast in Barbados, causing great offence. The decision was defended on the grounds that the news was old by then and could have been heard earlier on shortwave, an attitude some might have found arrogant.

But whatever judgement is made will be free of ideological pressure; it will stand or fall by purely journalistic standards. The World Service is required to provide a 'credible, unbiased, reliable, accurate, balanced and independent service of news covering international and national developments.' It has been argued, mostly by people with no experience of a radio newsroom, that the objectivity which this suggests is not possible, since the prejudices of the journalists will show, even if they are unconscious of them. In fact, men and women of very different temperaments and sympathies can work together to produce a perfectly objective news bulletin because they are professionals,

The newsroom today, still the heart of the World Service.

trained to do that within a tradition going back for over 60 years ('Give both sides').

Writing for radio news is a skill whose basics can be learned fairly quickly, although perhaps it needs a certain cast of mind. But success requires more than the basics. Impartiality sounds simple enough, but there are pitfalls. To call somebody a freedom fighter is to appear to take his side; call him a terrorist and you're against him. How about calling him a guerrilla, which, of course, sounds like gorilla but seems a nice neutral word? Do guerrillas leave bombs in supermarkets to kill indiscriminately? This is not a theoretical argument. For example, in the past there have been bitter complaints from listeners in Israel about the words used in World Service news to describe the actions of militant Palestinians (*militant*, now there's another dangerous word).

A newsroom guide issued to newcomers lists a number of words which should be used with care or avoided altogether – *tribesmen*, *natives*, *so-called*, *alleged*, for example. *Collide* is dangerous; it suggests liability. *Crisis* is often an overworked word, so is *massive*. Police should not be described as being *forced* to open fire. As the guide says, that's their story. People, dogs and ships are *missing*, they do not *go missing*. The guide is to be updated, and it is to be hoped that other phrases which sometimes sully the airwaves may be included: 'face to face meeting', for instance, as if there could be any other sort (back to bac ?), 'moderate' (applied to right-wing members of a left-wing organisation), 'scenario', 'quantum leap' – the list is enormous. The guide contains practical, commonsense advice, but you have no time to consult it when it is four o'clock in the morning and you have to write an urgent story about a bomb explosion at a summit meeting. So sometimes its precepts are forgotten.

Accuracy is another problem. John Gordon, a former editor of the *Sunday Express*, once said that when a member of the public reads in his newspaper a story with which he is familiar, he will discover mistakes. Journalists are at the mercy of their sources. News agency accounts of an incident may differ in detail. How to know which is correct? A mistake can make the service look ridiculous in the place where the news is coming from, and it loses credibility. One of the first lessons for a newcomer is learning to read news agency copy carefully, noticing the discrepancies between them and discounting the glosses.

It is particularly difficult in the case of upheavals – coups, revolutions, civil wars. As one exasperated news agency reporter in Bangladesh put it in the aftermath of the Indo-Pakistan war of 1971: 'The most difficult thing to find in this country is a fact.' In the absence of verifiable facts and in the face of competition there is a temptation to take risks and put out stories that are later shown to be untrue. But if the BBC uses the stories, it, not the news agency, has to take the blame. There was an example of this in the early sixties. Reuter reported the arrival of the then UN Secretary-General, Dag Hammarskjöld, at the town in the Belgian Congo (now Zaire) he was due to visit during the fighting which followed independence. But Reuter simply assumed he had arrived; in fact, his aircraft crashed and he was killed. The BBC was criticised for falsely reporting his arrival.

As a general rule – although there are exceptions – the newsroom requires two independent sources for a story. This does not necessarily mean just two news agencies.

The assassination of Rajiv Gandhi was reported by all the news agencies, but their information came from a single source, the Press Trust of India. Since it had not always proved reliable in the past, the story was held up – very briefly – until confirmation came from the BBC's own stringer. Incidentally, Rajiv Gandhi himself heard of his mother's

Listening to the BBC, Rajiv Gandhi, in Calcutta in 1984, hears of his mother's assassination.

assassination first from the BBC, because All-India radio held up the news while it debated how it should be handled – not quite the same thing.

When important news of this nature breaks there is a lot of action. First, it is 'snapped' into any bulletin that happens to be on the air. If it is really important it may even be flashed into a programme between news bulletins. A fuller version, with some background, will be quickly prepared, drawing if necessary on the resources of the cuttings library known as News Information. A headline will be issued, and the story will be frequently re-written to incorporate fresh developments. Re-writing can lead to mistakes. Qualifying phrases may be dropped, reports hardened to become facts. There was once a story which after several re-writes ended by quoting a BBC correspondent as saying the opposite of what he actually had said.

Since the war the BBC has built up an impressive corps of foreign correspondents –

more than any other media organisation in Britain. Their role, too, has evolved over the years. At one time, when many of them seemed to be former intelligence officers with the Eighth Army, they were not allowed to be first with the news. That was for the news agencies; the job of the correspondent was to provide expert analysis. So if a correspondent did get an exclusive story he had to pass it to a local news agency correspondent before he could use it .

With the growth of television the call went out for journalists of a different breed, those who, as one editor put it, 'could fight with Italian cameramen'. One of them is said to have actually done so during a foreign tour by the Pope, shouting: 'We beat you at ****** Monte Cassino and we'll beat you again!' – picturesque, if historically inaccurate. When news 'sequence' programmes became all the rage on Radio 4 in the seventies correspondents were so much in demand, with five different sequences, news bulletins, *Radio Newsreel* and perhaps television after their services, that they had very little time actually to look for news and were at times reduced to re-writing news agency copy.

The wheel has turned, if not full circle then at least part of the way and correspondents are now expected to provide both news and expert analysis. But the pressure can still be great. One correspondent, for example, wrote and broadcast no fewer than 18 despatches for different outlets in one day. Prodigious feats of this sort have been made possible by an improvement in communications. In the past correspondents relied on radio circuits which had to be booked about a day in advance and involved their attendance at a studio, an inflexible procedure which took no account of the actual news situation.

Nowadays they can simply pick up a telephone and, with the help of specialised equipment, deliver their reports in good sound quality – alhough not yet from all parts of the world.

Being part of the BBC as a whole gives Bush House resources that its competitors cannot match. It has access to everything in the output – despatches from correspondents, material from domestic radio and television, for example. An interview with a visiting statesman on, say, *Panorama* can be heard by the whole world. It also has its own correspondents, some abroad, some at home. The London-based correspondents are grouped in a Correspondents' Unit, which began life as a Political Intelligence Unit, in day-to-day touch with the Foreign Office. Its quasi-diplomatic function has long since gone; it is now a purely journalistic enterprise with correspondents covering such subjects as politics, defence, diplomatic and economic affairs. The argument is that a great deal of material needs to be specially written for overseas listeners whose background is different from those at home.

Their knowledge of Britain and British ways is much less, and more has to be explained. English idioms alone can be puzzling: what

would a foreigner make of such phrases as a *sticky wicket, no axe to grind, the curate's egg,* for example ?

World Service news is lucky to have a great deal of expertise at its disposal in the form of the language services. They can often elucidate an apparently puzzling development in their own countries and explain its significance. It also has its team of overseas stringers, part-time correspondents who fill gaps in places where there is no full-time correspondent. Some are employed by the newsroom, others by the various services. The African service, for example, has its own stringers in most African countries.

Life for them can be dangerous. A white, Western journalist may be expelled if he or she offends the authorities. That is unpleasant enough, but if you are a local journalist there are worse fates. A Ghanaian was detained for months without trial and tortured because of his reporting for the BBC. Towards the end of the Indo-Pakistan war in 1971, when Indian soldiers were closing in on Dhaka, capital of what is now Bangladesh, supporters of Pakistan were infuriated by the BBC because it was reporting Pakistani defeats. They went to the home of the BBC stringer, a Bengali, who was not responsible for the reports, dragged him out into the street and murdered him in front of his wife and children. In 1987 the BBC stringer in Nairobi suffered spinal damage when a Kenyan policeman broke a club across her back. It takes courage to be a correspondent in these circumstances; they deserve great praise. According to the head of the African service, Dorothy Grenfell Williams, the service could not exist without its stringers: 'We are making journalism respectable, in the way it should be in Africa, by having these people.'

World Service news has traditionally consisted of a bulletin of a little under ten minutes in length read by a single newsreader without the recorded contributions from correspondents which practically every other broadcaster uses. The rationale is that, for people whose first language is not English, listening perhaps under difficult reception conditions, this was easier to understand. Bulletins of this type continue, but 'illustrated' bulletins including inserts were introduced during the Gulf War.

The newsroom has sometimes underplayed important stories emanating from Britain, relegating them to *News about Britain* or even ignoring them altogether. This is because of an attitude of mind suggesting that many such items are 'not World Service stories' – too trivial, perhaps or, in the ironical words of the present editor of World Service news, Bob Jobbins, 'not boring enough.' He says things have improved: 'The question is whether it is the sort of story a foreign correspondent based in London would send back to his own organisation.'

It has also tended to be over-conscious of its serious role, leading it to concentrate rather too often on reporting statements about international politics to the exclusion of stories that might be more interesting and, in the long run, more significant. 'The United Nations Secretary-General has said the Middle East crisis will only be solved by

mutual agreement' is a parody of a World Service headline, but not, I think, a gross one. (However, this bland sort of headline has been less common in the last few years.)

Of course, statements about international politics can be important, but what people do is usually more revealing than what they say, and it is possible to exaggerate their importance. Group summit meetings, for example, are valuable to the extent that they enable busy world leaders to discuss common problems.

But the world leaders themselves are becoming increasingly adept at using the media for their own ends and take advantage of summits to boost their prestige with the folks back home. They are really rather expensive television productions.

One of the minor curses of the age is the propensity to issue high-sounding declarations at these meetings, which are immediately forgotten. In spite of all the attention given by the media to these circuses – and they are covered by hundreds of journalists – the world is not greatly changed by them.

But, to take a few random examples, new methods of contraception, the changing relationship between men and women in the West, the development of communications –

Unsolicited testimonial: a cartoon from the Times of India *in July, 1986.*

radio, television and video – the increasing destitution of the Third World and the large-scale movements of populations from there to the affluent West, all these are affecting our lives to a far greater extent than political statements, so often featured in news bulletins.

This argument cannot, of course, be pressed too far; its logical outcome would be an entirely different definition of news and, in any case, it is not always easy to identify developments which hold significance for the future. On the analogy of the first BBC Arabic broadcast, the crucifixion might have rated a mention in the Roman World Service, particularly in its Aramaic transmission, doubtless followed by complaints from Pontius Pilate. But it would not have been immediately seen as an event that was to change history.

However, it is not a bad idea to remind ourselves from time to time that events that are accorded the most media attention are not always the most important. What was more significant in 1922, for example – the international conference to discuss German reparations for the First World War or the publication of Eliot's 'The Waste Land'?

Most listeners to the World Service are men; women are apparently less interested in news, at least in the form in which it is now presented. Bush House as a whole is trying to attract more women listeners. Two-thirds of the people in the Third World countries it broadcasts to are below the age of 20. Women and young people perhaps need a different diet. 'We don't get to grips with science or the arts,' says Bob Jobbins. But things are changing, and a more varied fare is being offered to existing as well as potential listeners. World Service news broadcast an item about the last episode of the American soap opera Dallas, something unthinkable in earlier days but justified by the fact that countless millions all over the world have watched it. Not epoch-making, perhaps, but

the very existence of television soap operas with a worldwide audience is a significant modern phenomenon.

There has been an expansion of news and current affairs over the past few years along with an increase in the amount of material. The number of despatches from correspondents has risen by three-quarters, news agency copy by a half. The world has seen an extraordinary succession of events. 'There are times,' says Bob Jobbins, 'when you think the world can't cope with any more international incidents, and then you find yourself faced with the cyclone disaster in Bangladesh, the assassination of Rajiv Gandhi and the Kremlin putsch, whose failure was communism's last gasp. We have been living on adrenalin for so long, I can't imagine what 'ordinary' news would be like.' (Nation to Nation, BBC 1991)

But although the amount of news has increased so greatly, the principles of reporting it have not changed. A young man applying for a job in Bush House many years ago was asked how he would treat a news item that reflected badly on Britain. 'I would judge it only on its news value,' he said, adding after what seemed an ominous pause: 'That may be the wrong answer, but that's what I should do.' And, of course, it was the right answer and he got the job. Nothing has changed in that respect. Many years later, in 1991, the World Service gave the same treatment to a report by Amnesty International criticising abuses of human rights in Britain as it had when the finger was pointed at other countries.

The former Director-General Sir William Haley, made the point just after the war: 'The British conception of news as something coldly impersonal and objective, having as its only touchstone accuracy, impartiality and truth, is one of our great services to a civilisation in which speed of communication gives news an overwhelming importance it never had before.'

CHAPTER ELEVEN

Self Satisfied and Self Congratulatory?

ONE DAY in the late seventies the British High Commissioner in Lagos received an official complaint about the BBC World Service. It was neither the first, nor the last, but unusually it was nothing to do with news or current affairs, it was over a phrase in a religious talk. The speaker, a canon of St. Paul's, had recently seen General Gowon deposed as Nigeria's military leader in 1975 and living in England. Gowon, he said, had suffered for his Christian belief. The Nigerian military government saw this comment as offensive because Gowon's successor was a Muslim.

Episodes like this are more common than most people realise, with an average of one complaint a month said to be a conservative estimate. Governments complain for a variety of reasons, but perceived bias is perhaps the main one. Those with an imperfect grasp of democracy object when opposition politicians silenced in their own country find a platform on the World Service. They complain of interference in their internal affairs. The BBC replies that it tries to get balancing comment from government spokesmen but they are not always willing or able to provide it.

During the Gulf War governments in the

Allied coalition sometimes made official complaints at a high level at what they saw as pro-Iraqi bias on the part of the BBC Arabic service. This was because news bulletins would report Iraqi statements in some detail without any response from the Allied side. There was no response immediately available, but the BBC does not conceal news on those grounds. It reported the Iraqi statements for what they were worth, as part of the general picture. Allied statements were reported when they were made. This even-handed approach is not always appreciated; it has its critics in Britain too. But journalists are not in a position to judge the truth of conflicting statements and therefore give both sides, as Reith recommended all those years ago. Rebuttals of statements by opponents are usually the job of government or military spokesmen, not the BBC.

But there have been times when the BBC has actively sought rebuttals. At the beginning of the 1967 Arab-Israel war President Nasser of Egypt accused Britain of giving military help to Israel, an accusation supported by King Hussein of Jordan. As the proverb has it, a lie is halfway round the world before the truth has got its boots on, and this accusation could have led to all sorts of dire consequences, anti-British riots, death and destruction. Bush House looked for a British comment at the highest level and within hours received a firm denial from the then Foreign Secretary, George Brown.

When they receive protests about the BBC ambassadors and high commissioners (in Commonwealth countries) have a standard reply: 'We are not responsible for the media in Britain', a reply which is received with polite incredulity in most cases. The protesting governments very often have no difficulty in controlling their own media, and they know that the Foreign Office pays for the World Service. So how can it not be responsible?

Protests are referred back to the FCO which in turn passes them on to the BBC. The diplomats abroad may sometimes endorse them. As a member of the Foreign Office put it: 'It's no secret that some diplomats overseas tend to associate themselves more with the country they're in than with their own country. And it's rather difficult if you are called out of bed at midnight and dragged to the presidential dinner to be given a dressing down about the BBC. You tend to be rather acidic in reporting it the next morning.... And you may have gone through a particularly difficult bilateral period and be just emerging from the gloom and – dammit, the BBC broadcasts something that upsets them; that's six or nine months work down the drain because they will insist the BBC is part of government.'

It is not only foreigners who believe the World Service is controlled by the Foreign Office; many people in Britain assume it. What are the facts? The first is that it is part of the BBC as a whole, subject to the same freedoms and constraints. In theory the government can require the BBC to broadcast or refrain from broadcasting anything it likes; in practice this does not happen.

The second fact is that the World Service has particular obligations to the government.

Under the terms of the Licence Agreement the Corporation 'shall send programmes...to such countries, in such languages and at such times as, after consultation with the Corporation, may from time to time be prescribed.....' This, of course, is the formula from the 1946 White Paper, as is the other specific obligation: 'The Corporation shall consult and collaborate with the department specified and shall obtain and accept from them such information regarding conditions in, and the policies of Her Majesty's Government towards the countries so prescribed and other countries as will enable the Corporation to plan and prepare its programmes in the External Services in the national interest.'

This has been interpreted incorrectly as meaning that the World Service has to give news about Britain when it is not strictly relevant: 'Being obliged to include information about policies and life in Britain sometimes leads to editorial decisions not being made on purely newsworthy grounds.' (*Media Diplomacy*, by Yoel Cohen, Frank Cass and Company, 1986). This is simply nonsense, based on a misunderstanding of what the words 'obtain and accept' mean in practice. They refer to the distribution of some FCO telegrams to senior staff in Bush House, the simplest way of providing information about foreign countries.

The mention of telegrams has a slightly sinister air, as if reading a despatch from an ambassador is likely to brainwash the innocent reader into accepting all the views of the Foreign Office. But they are mostly factual and are looked on as sources of information, supplementing other sources, not as policy guidance. FCO telegrams are also shown to others, including diplomatic correspondents of the national press and radio at the regular briefings for them organised by the FCO.

The requirement to consult and collaborate is nowadays interpreted fairly

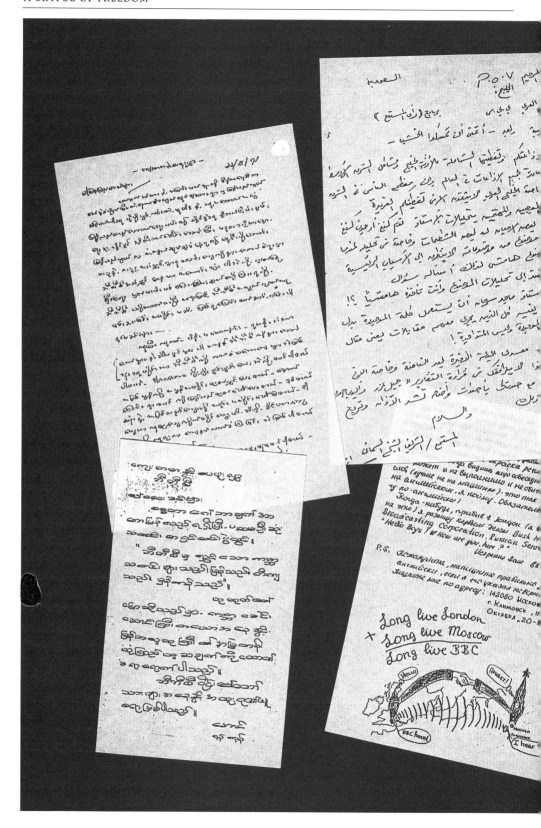

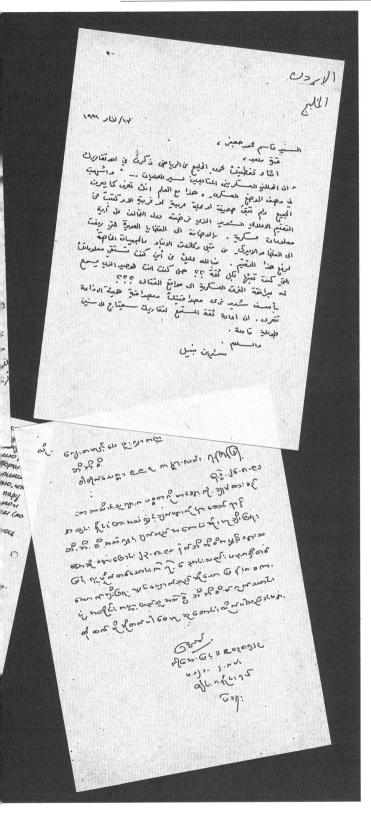

loosely. When the foreign language services were still new, immediately before and during the war, there was, as we have seen, a good deal of consultation between the Foreign Office and the BBC. This continued for some time after the war. Certain services, Arabic, for example, and Far Eastern, had regular briefings with the desk officers for their particular areas. But this did not mean that they simply took orders – on the contrary. After the 1967 Arab-Israeli war a Foreign Office information officer told members of the Arabic Service at their briefing that their job was now to help topple Nasser. Members of the Arabic Service know as much about the Middle East as diplomats do, and it was intimated to him politely that this was not how they saw it, and they took no notice. Soon afterwards their stance was justified: British policy changed and Nasser became the least of the various problems of the Middle East.

Nowadays there are no special regular meetings of this nature, although the Bush House diplomatic correspondent attends the daily briefing for all diplomatic correspondents. The FCO encourages its geographical departments to have contacts with the equivalent language services. This is seen as being of mutual benefit. The Information Department also maintains contacts with Bush House, dealing, among other things, with complaints. But the Foreign Office insists that it has no editorial control at all. Simply listening to the World Service makes that plain; the only broadcasts made at the behest of the FCO are occasional messages advising British subjects about what to do in places where tension is high, and these are clearly labelled.

Listeners' letters from Burma, Russia and The Gulf: 'Most people in the Middle East trust only your coverage.' (Saudi Arabia). 'I say with great regret that the truthfulness and credibility of the BBC have been lost.' (Jordan). 'The old Burmese saying is true: "The criticism of a thousand fools is dissolved by the wise man's praise." ...the BBC is loved by the world's people.' (Burma).

What seems to have happened is a process of evolution over 60 years. People working for what is now the World Service have been proud of their independence and sought to maintain it. Many have said they would leave if they were subject to Foreign Office control. In 1985, the BBC governors agreed to a request from the Home Secretary to postpone the showing of a television programme about Northern Ireland. BBC journalists staged a 24-hour strike in protest. The strike was strongly supported in Bush House, whose staff felt betrayed; after boasting of their freedom from government control, they were now (as they saw it) giving in to government pressure – a gift to their critics.

For their part the diplomats have come to see that the independence of the BBC, embarrassing though it may be at times, is ultimately to their benefit. British prestige is enhanced by a radio service which tells the truth, even if it is not always palatable. It would be impossible to find nowadays another Rex Leeper arguing for 'an innocent form of propaganda', leaving out unhelpful items – at least it would not be argued in public.

That is not to say that all members of the diplomatic service are happy with what they hear. One former high commissioner, who had several brushes with the BBC over its output, was reported to have said that he didn't mind where he was posted next as long as it was somewhere he couldn't receive it. And one or two people in the Foreign Office in the past argued that it was absurd that the World Service should be financed through them and yet be free from scrutiny; its output should be checked for conformity with British Government policy. But that was the opinion of individuals, not official policy.

There have been two publicly described occasions when the World Service has agreed to a government request not to broadcast a programme as planned. On the eve of the Arab-Israeli war of 1967 the Soviet Union threatened to break off talks with the Foreign Secretary, George Brown, if the Russian service went ahead with its reading from a book by Stalin's daughter, Svetlana, who had fled to the West. Since the talks had been arranged to try to avert the war the BBC agreed at the highest level to postpone the broadcast. But the talks were unsuccessful, George Brown returned to London, and the broadcast went ahead forty-eight hours later. The second time was in 1975 when Idi Amin was in power in Uganda. The Foreign Office persuaded Bush House management that broadcasting a review of a book about him by a British expatriate would infuriate him and so endanger the lives of Britons in Uganda. Again the broadcast was postponed, only to be transmitted three weeks later with no ill effects.

After the government of what was then Rhodesia unilaterally declared independence in 1965 the government asked the BBC to mount a special programme for white Rhodesians to bring home to them their isolation and the consequences of their government's action. The government set up a 50 kilowatt medium wave transmitter at Francistown in Botswana, near the Rhodesian border, together with a low-power short wave transmitter. A special programme called 'The World and Rhodesia' was transmitted several times a day. The Rhodesian authorities jammed it, it became increasingly difficult to hear and a British journalist reported that 'even among sympathisers with what the BBC are doing there is a fairly general feeling that the programmes are propaganda.' It was brought to an end in 1968. In the words of Gerard Mansell: '...the operation did not succeed in its object, as was perhaps inevitable, and the BBC had come close – some felt too close – to allowing itself to be used for a purpose which some regarded as lying well outside its proper function.' (*Let Truth be Told*, Gerard Mansell, Weidenfeld and Nicolson, 1982)

One country in which the BBC was taken very seriously was the Soviet Union during

At his home in Vermont, Alexander Solzhenitsyn talks to Janis Sapiets, BBC East European current-affairs specialist.

what is now known as the years of stagnation. In 1979 two Soviet authors wrote a monograph about it. It is, of course, written from a Marxist viewpoint, which makes it an historical document, but its interest lies in the fact that it is probably the only detailed critical account of Bush House output in any language.

Parts of the monograph were translated by David Wedgwood Benn of Bush House, and one thing that emerges is the fact that the authors attributed their own motives to the BBC. For example (they said) it falsely reported the death of President Makarios in the Cyprus coup in 1974 because Britain had military bases on the island and its partition was to the advantage of 'certain circles in Great Britain'. The coup was mounted by supporters of union with Greece, encouraged by the colonels who were in power there. It led to their downfall and to the Turkish invasion of the island in defence of the Turkish Cypriots, which did actually lead to de facto partition. But the BBC was innocent. For the first few hours after the coup Makarios was believed to be dead. In fact, he had

escaped and was finally rescued by a British military helicopter; there were no hidden motives in the report.

The essential argument of the monograph was that the so-called objectivity of the BBC was really a process of subtle distortion. It acknowledged its 'gentlemanly tones' in comparison to the 'crude anti-communism' of the American stations. But this, of course, was just part of its cunning. And the authors described a BBC programme to show just how cunning it was: 'In a lengthy programme on the energy crisis in Great Britain only two or three minutes were devoted to an analysis of the crisis phenomena. Most of the broadcast was concerned with new methods of obtaining energy. There was a description of the drilling of oil on the bed of the North Sea, its extraction from shales, the use of solar energy and finally the development of nuclear power and the 'excellent working' of British atomic power stations. As a result the broadcast emerged as a panegyric of British technology.'

The authors also accused the BBC of

Santanan Swaminathia, of the BBC's Tamil language programme, with the latest batch of letters from listeners.

portraying Northern Ireland in consistently more favourable terms than Britain's own press. The situation in Northern Ireland has, in fact, often been used by overseas critics of the World Service who say in effect: 'How can you criticise what you are pleased to call our repression of violent dissidents when you are doing the same thing in your country?' Some people in Bush House would argue that it has not done a very good reporting job. In the words of one member of staff: 'It's not for political reasons, it's simply a mindset. You tend to disregard what's going on in your own bailliwick. We don't think it's important, but to people out there there's a war going on in Northern Ireland. Someone's being killed practically every day. If this had been going on in, say, Belgium, we'd be reporting it every day.'

Some of the severest criticism of the work

of the World Service comes from within its own ranks. The criticism can be spontaneous, born of concern that a particular department has made a serious error of judgement. There was one such case in 1978 when a rebellion in southern Zaire put the lives of several thousand civilians in the town of Kolwezi in danger. There is, said the World Service news, growing concern for the fate of the white civilians in Kolwezi; no mention was made of black civilians who were equally at risk. This was the tone of the reporting throughout. The World Service, of course, had to depend on the news agencies and the BBC correspondents on the spot, but it is after all widely listened to in Africa and might have been expected to show a more imaginative attitude.

A member of the African service was so incensed by the coverage that he wrote a lengthy memorandum. He said that one reason there was never any serious discussion about mistakes in news and current affairs coverage 'lies, I believe, in the tendency to be self-satisfied and self-congratulatory.' He described the reporting of the affair as racist, with the use of such emotive words and phrases in despatches from correspondents as 'savage', 'reports of widespread rape' and 'tribesmen'. And he mentioned comments from listeners personally known to him. 'There is a widespread view,' he said, 'that the BBC, along with the rest of the British media, completely failed to give fair, objective and informative news about what was going on. They also compared the coverage with the way we report wars and conflicts elsewhere to back up their views that we change our news values when the lives of white people are at stake.'

Self-satisfied and self-congratulatory? There is something in the charge. Complacency has always been a danger in Bush House, partly because it receives so much praise and partly because it does not hesitate to praise itself.

There was a small but revelatory incident in 1991, after President Gorbachev had been held prisoner in the Crimea during the short-lived coup. He said he had been able to listen to foreign radios, and the BBC was the best. The wording suggested he was talking about its reception, not the contents, but the subsequent BBC publicity gave a different impression. A newspaper advertisement showed Mr Gorbachev at his desk. Underneath were the words: 'When you need to know what's going on in the world.' A retired member of the newsroom wrote a sceptical letter to the staff newspaper, *Ariel*: 'Before this tribute becomes enshrined in BBC mythology perhaps you could ask Monitoring to tell us exactly what Gorbachev said. Just in the interests of impartial reporting. Or do the interests of self-publicity take precedence nowadays?'

The Monitoring service duly obliged and made it clear that Gorbachev was indeed referring to the reception of the BBC, not making a judgement about its programmes. He described how his guards were able to rig up aerials and went on: 'They got the BBC best (laughter and applause). The BBC sounded best, Radio Liberty, then Voice of America appeared...'. The Prime Minister, John Major, did write to Bush House praising its coverage of the attempted coup, and, as we shall see later, there were other tributes to the BBC coverage. But on this occasion it was, if anything, the audibility that was being praised.

A British listener with a knowledge of Russian wrote: 'Come off it, BBC,' but, judging by the comments of others, the tribute has in fact become 'enshrined in mythology.'

Perhaps the view that Britain enjoys the best of all possible world-services springs partly from a perceived need for Bush House to justify itself to the government and the taxpayer. Ever since the war it has been under pressure, faced with the possibility and sometimes the reality of cuts in services. Senior executives spend a great deal of time not broadcasting but arguing its case, in public lectures, to MPs, to the FCO. Everybody (or nearly everybody) pats it on the back, but when there are to be cuts in public expenditure it is liable to suffer. So it seizes every opportunity to congratulate itself to show the authorities what a valuable asset it is to Britain.

The more positive aspect is a sense of purpose. Like the rest of the BBC, Bush House is top-heavy in management, but its atmosphere is different. People of many nationalities work together; the staff restaurant and club could be part of the United Nations, except that the staff get on with one another rather better. Many of them are speaking to their own countrymen and women, sometimes providing them with a rare link to the outside world.

They know the work they are doing is valuable and deserves recognition. So it does, and it is through publicity that it is increasingly receiving that recognition in Britain.

When it reports wars and conflicts elsewhere the World Service usually manages to upset one side, normally the side that is losing. During the Indo-Pakistan war of 1971 BBC correspondents in Pakistan were confronted by enraged people who accused it of being the Bharat (i.e. Indian) Broadcasting Corporation. Their own media were reporting Pakistani victories; the BBC was reporting Pakistani defeats. They assumed it was lying. The consequences to the BBC stringer in Dhaka has already been mentioned; the fate of the correspondents in Pakistan was not so drastic, but they had some nasty moments.

By contrast, the World Service was greeted with acclamation in Bangladesh, created by the victory of the Indian army. It had reported the sufferings of the country, in the devastating cyclone of 1970 and later under the occupation of the Pakistan army. It was seen as a friend, and huge numbers of ordinary people listened to it, even taking their transistor radios with them when they went

out, so as not to miss the Bengali transmission in the evening. In an article in 1972 headed 'Friends, we remember you' the Morning News of Bangladesh had this to say:

'Owing to its unflagging interest in the suffering millions of the people of Bangladesh, the services done and sympathy shown towards our people, BBC has become so much popular that the term BBC has become a household word with the people of Bangladesh. Even in the remote rural areas where people never understand what the term BBC actually stands for they too switch on their radio set just in time to listen to the BBC *Calling Asia* programme (Bengali).'

This is all very heart-warming, but the idea that the BBC is a friend of Bangladesh (or anywhere else) is based on a misconception. The logic, often used by people after successful 'liberation' struggles is: the BBC reports news which is favourable to our cause, therefore the BBC is on our side. But the BBC does not take sides; it broadcasts the news available to it, and if the events favour one side, then that is what it reports. I can recall a personal example of how the messenger is confused with the message, dating from this period in Bangladesh. Roy Jenkins, at that time foreign affairs spokesman for the Labour Party, paid a visit and when he left gave a news conference in the course of which he said the British government should recognise the new country. I duly reported this and a few days later one of my Bengali contacts said: 'I hear you've been saying the British government should recognise us.'

The trouble with this 'the BBC is our friend' attitude is that it usually ends in tears when circumstances change and it starts reporting the bad news. The government of Bangladesh, so fulsome at the time of liberation, later turned hostile. In 1987, for instance, it expelled the BBC correspondent and forbade anyone to communicate news to the Corporation because of its reporting of opposition to the then President Ershad.

But the people still listen to the Bengali service, particularly at times of crisis.

The BBC knows that people listen because it carries out audience surveys through independent polling organisations in most countries.

There are several where it has not been possible to take polls – China, for example, Burma, Afghanistan, Iran – and the global figure of 120 million regular listeners does not include them. The figure sounds impressive – 120 million people listening at least once a week, many more than the domestic services can command, even including television. But it needs to be put into perspective; it represents only 2.3 per cent of the world's total population. In other words, the overwhelming majority never listen to and very probably have never even heard of the BBC.

Many of those who do write to London – over 537,000 in 1990. Often, of course, they are requesting programme details or taking part in competitions or other forms of listener participation. But sometimes they express their opinions of the BBC, as the following examples show:

From India to the English service: 'I am very disappointed for the lack of ball-by-ball cricket commentary. Your commentary builds up our English knowledge, pronunciation and the pleasure of listening.'

From Germany to the Turkish service: 'We listen to all your broadcasts with keen interest and pleasure. Being prisoners in a German jail we make great use of your medical programmes and we appreciate hearing some good genuine Turkish music...'

From Tanzania to the Swahili service: 'For anybody black or white to accuse the BBC of revealing government secrets is a sign of ignorance. It is like playing a guitar and asking a goat to dance to the music.'

From Saudi Arabia to the Indonesian service: 'I think you should make more

efforts to encourage more Indonesians living in Saudi Arabia to listen to the BBC news. It is like a good morning meal which one does not want to miss every morning.'

From China to the Chinese service: 'All through the years your meticulous detailed News Report always starts at the beginning and other programmes follow. After rearranging the programmes we have the news summary at the beginning but we have to sit and wait for 30 minutes for the detailed news. This....style is like a fish bone stuck in the throat, you wish to swallow it rather than hold it back feeling. The waiting is torture and has a blackmailed feeling.'

From Saudi Arabia to the Thai service: 'The number of Thai people in my firm who listen to the BBC is around 30. I don't know about other firms, but I've given them the programme guides.....By the way, I was in complete agreement that the BBC should be nominated for a Nobel Prize.'

From Japan to the Japanese service: 'Frankly speaking, I was taken by surprise at the news that the BBC Japanese service is going to be terminated... I have learned many things through the BBC programmes, above all how to analyse the given information. Therefore I expected to make the most of BBC reports in the years to come. I am disappointed at the decision.'

From Brazil to the Latin American (Brazilian) service: 'To me to listen to the short wave is like sailing in a sea where one never sailed before. To me this is a sheer pleasure, although sometimes reception is not very good and comes along with some interference. This means that my sister who is close by gets irritated. She is indeed a pain in the neck, but I do not mind. To me the BBC is more than my sister, as tuning in to the BBC is like being there in London. Many thanks.'

CHAPTER TWELVE

The Impact of the World Service

THE FACT that so many foreign governments complain about BBC broadcasts shows they have an impact; there would be little point in complaining if nobody took any notice of them. The effect of one series of broadcasts on the military government in Ghana has already been described in the Introduction to this book. There have been a number of similar cases when rulers have blamed the BBC at least in part for encompassing their downfall. This chapter relates some of them, in particular the stories of Iran, Vietnam and Liberia.

The Shah of Iran was convinced that the BBC had engineered the downfall of his father in 1941 and that it was hostile to him personally. This was partly because the BBC did not take his pretensions as seriously as he would have liked. The journalist Hazhir Teimourian, who was a member of the service, recalled that 'for years, its broadcasters – about a dozen full-time men and women – had refused to bow to Iranian pressure to refer to the Shah in adulatory terms, particularly his most frequently used title of 'Light of the Aryans', and they had given coverage to critical, as well as supportive, accounts of the Shah's conduct.'

(From *The Times* on the 50th anniversary of the Persian Service, January 1991)

In 1978, at the Shah's prompting, the government of Iraq expelled Ayatollah Khomeini, who had been preaching against him in the holy city of Najaf unheard by the outside world.

From the Shah's point of view it was a terrible mistake. The Ayatollah turned up in Paris and immediately had access to the world's media.

As revolutionary turmoil grew in Iran the BBC Persian service found itself being blamed for encouraging it. It was accused of broadcasting instructions in bomb making and guerrilla warfare techniques and of acting as spokesman for the Ayatollah Khomeini, thereby rallying support for anti-Shah demonstrations and marches. The output of the service was subjected to intense scrutiny and no evidence was found for any of the allegations.

In fact, as Hazhir Teimourian wrote, during the last month of the Shah's rule the BBC service interviewed his last prime minister, Dr Shahpour Bakhtiar, three times while the Ayatollah was interviewed only once during all his months of exile in Paris – 'yet we were subsequently blamed by many Iranians for somehow engineering the revolution for the purposes of British imperialism.'

And not only Iranians. One of the curious features of this episode is the way British businessmen, politicians and journalists were drawn in to what was clearly a deliberate attempt to discredit the service. Those visiting Iran were handed what purported to be transcripts of its broadcasts; these were investigated in London and proved not to have been broadcast at all. But they were convincing enough to fool some people. The

former Foreign Secretary, Lord George Brown, went on Capital Radio in November 1978 to slam them as 'tendentious, disruptive, partial and provocative' and putting British businessmen and diplomats at risk. The reply by the managing director, Gerard Mansell, the following week was unambiguous: 'Utter rubbish!'

The Shah and his entourage seem to have become paranoid about the BBC. One of his generals asked an official American visitor if the United States could stop the broadcasts. There were even plans to sabotage the

In 1951, at the height of the oil crisis, British oilmen in Abadan listen to the latest news from the world outside.

transmitters in Cyprus and Masirah, eventually vetoed by the Shah. It was official British policy to support his regime, and there was great pressure on the service. The British Embassy in Teheran found it a nuisance and would have like to see it close.

The Foreign Office, to its credit, refused to interfere, although it relayed the complaints to the BBC and emphasised the need to be accurate and objective. The chairman and secretary of the Anglo-Iranian Parliamentary Group – both Conservative MPs – studied the text of the broadcasts and agreed that they showed no evidence of bias against the Shah.

Indeed, they included a statement from the then Foreign Secretary, Dr David Owen, strongly supporting him and giving a warning that the alternative was rule by 'fanatical Muslims'.

The Shah fell in January 1979. He had blamed the Persian service because a lot of people listened to it. Sir Anthony Parsons, British ambassador in Teheran at the time and a critic of the service, later conceded that it had not been at fault. In a broadcast on Radio 4 in 1984 he said it had reported perfectly fairly by telling the people of Iran in their own language things that were actually happening in their country which their own authorities were disguising from them.

It turned out that the new rulers of Iran had no more time for the Persian service than had their predecessors. After they had taken over they executed large numbers of people, allegedly 'agents' of the Shah, and the BBC reported the protests from the out-side world. Teheran Radio in a commentary in May 1979 evidently decided that attack was the best form of defence:

'Radio London, which seems to be the throat of the banks, the international monopolies and the big capital, soaked with the blood of the nations, has with sarcasm and a vicious sting, resorted to blaming and

reproaching our revolution. The professional philanthropists have pulled a vinegary face at the execution of criminals. Radio London refers to the recent revolutionary executions as being a barbarous act reminiscent of the stone age. But it prefers to remain silent about those stone age savages who imposed all the barbarism and brutishness of the cave-dwelling age on our society and tore to pieces the most patriotic and noblest women and men of this society in torture dungeons with fiendish instruments and techniques which were the direct product of the US, British and Israeli 'philanthropic' imperialists...Radio London, this mouthpiece of world-guzzling capitalism, which seems to continue to dream of that empire on which the sun never set, defends the torturers who used to torture the prisoners in order to whip up an appetite.' And so on, in the same vein.

The government of what was South Vietnam was another which sought to blame the BBC for its demise. In this case the complaint was that it gave details of a military withdrawal which subsequently became a rout.

The curious thing about Vietnam was that listening to the BBC Vietnamese service was widespread, although there had never been any considerable British presence there. The service began in 1952; by the seventies Gerald Priestland, later to become the BBC religious affairs correspondent, was able to report:

'Everyone seemed to listen to the BBC in Vietnam. No one took any notice when Hanoi, Saigon or the American Forces Network said a town was in danger; but if I or my BBC colleagues said it was, the entire population of the place would get up and go, brushing us aside as they fled. I remember standing in the main square in Saigon one morning, waiting for President Thieu to address his people from the rostrum, and hearing my own voice intoning from several hundred portable transistors tuned in to the

BBC Singapore station.' (*Something Understood*, Andre Deutsch 1986)

Lawrie Breen, who was Vietnamese programme organiser for over eight years and later became head of the Far East service, recalled some of the satisfaction he felt 'when I heard the familiar sounds of the BBC in Vietnamese through the open windows as I walked through the streets of the city of Hue in Central Vietnam one evening...' Nor was listening confined to the areas controlled from Saigon. 'An American woman journalist held captive for some time by a Vietnamese communist unit operating in Cambodia reported after her release that her captors never missed listening in to the daily news broadcasts from the BBC. And many years later General Vo-Nguyen Giap, who masterminded the Vietminh victory over the French at Dien Bien Phu in 1954 told a BBC visitor that he never failed to listen to the BBC throughout the war.'

The reason for this widespread listening was, of course, that the people did not trust their own media. Other countries broadcast in Vietnamese – the Americans, and the Australians, for example, and from the communist bloc Moscow and Peking. But they were seen as being committed to one side or the other; the BBC was seen as impartial, although the British government gave verbal, if not military, support to the US involvement.

In the last days of the war, in 1975, with the Americans long gone and South Vietnam facing defeat, the BBC was accused in general terms of releasing information which the communists could use as intelligence about troop movements. In particular President Thieu singled out a broadcast reporting the capture by the communists of some of the outposts along the Cambodian frontier. This had caused people to flee the area, hampering reinforcements which were unable to get through.

Was the complaint justified? The BBC was simply reporting the facts. And in the opinion of Lawrie Breen: 'The real question was whether the report had any long-term effect on the ability of the South Vietnamese to continue to resist, and I think it's fair to say that the South Vietnamese government was doomed anyway. I think the allegation is basically unfair and can't be sustained.'

But he does make the point that, while South Vietnam was relatively open to the media, so that any blemish could be reported, the communist north imposed strict, total censorship and so, unlike the south, was able to control the impression received by the outside world – an imbalance which exists in other confrontations between relatively open and closed societies.

For example, television viewers all over the world can regularly see on their screens Israeli soldiers mistreating Palestinians. But they will not see equally fierce treatment meted out by police in Arab countries, whose governments ensure that there are no cameras present.

The Vietnamese service was later criticised for allegedly encouraging refugees – the boat people – to seek asylum in a particular country. It was even claimed that it broadcast special weather reports to help them.

The complaints came from the countries affected. But, Lawrie Breen says, there was never any basis at all for the allegations: 'The only possible explanation for such stories, if they were not total fabrications, can have been that in certain instances people had heard in BBC broadcasts that a boatload of refugees had been allowed to land in a particular place and had decided to follow suit.'

The Liberian civil war of 1990 provided an extraordinary example of BBC influence, and its coverage resulted in perhaps the closest the BBC ever came to a saturation audience,

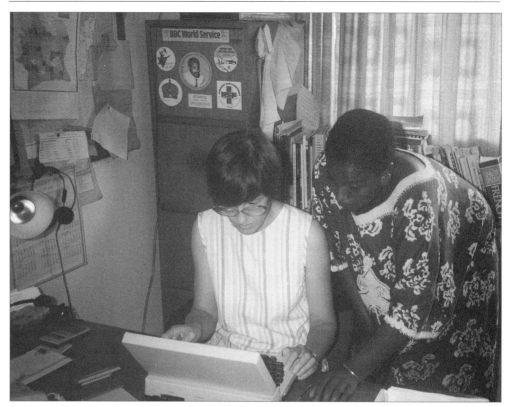

In Liberia, Elizabeth Blunt came close to death when her courageous reporting alerted the world to the Liberian coup. Here, she is in her office in Abidjan with her successor, Ofeibea Quist-Arcton.

Liberia was settled by freed American slaves in the nineteenth century and became an independent republic in 1847. It has long had close economic and cultural ties with the United States.

When Charles Taylor's men invaded the country at the head of an army to overthrow President Samuel Doe he telephoned the BBC in London and the Voice of America to announce the news.

The BBC West Africa correspondent, Elizabeth Blunt, based in Abidjan, capital of the Ivory Coast, was to pay six visits to Liberia after that to cover what developed into a sickening civil war – 'long enough to see the country change before my eyes from one of the more prosperous and amusing parts of West Africa into a smoking, bleeding shell.'

The Voice of America correspondent,

also based in Abidjan, did not pay one visit.

One can only speculate about the reasons. Perhaps the State Department did not want the war covered. But there is no doubt about the result.

Within two or three months VOA had lost its audience in Liberia to the BBC which was providing detailed coverage of the conflict to the country itself, the rest of Africa and the world.

This saturation coverage had an influence on the course of events. As the rebels drew nearer to the capital, Monrovia, the Liberian army began killing people who for tribal reasons they thought might be sympathetic to Taylor.

There was one particular massacre in which hundreds of people were killed as they lay asleep in what they thought was a place of safety, in the Lutheran church. President

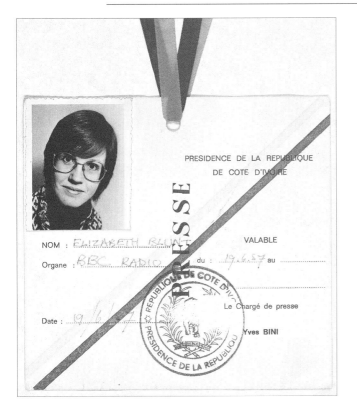

The press card of a BBC journalist can be a pass to welcome or, sometimes, mortal danger. This one, from the Ivory Coast, was held by Elizabeth Blunt.

Sir Dawda Jawara of The Gambia told Elizabeth Blunt later that when he heard her report on the massacre he came finally to the conclusion that a West African peace-keeping force would have to go into Liberia to try to stop the killing.

The Economic Community of West African States (ECOWAS) was holding a summit meeting in his capital, Banjul, at the time.

The peace-keeping force itself provided the backdrop to one of the more dramatic mass killings, by the followers of Prince Johnson, formerly one of Taylor's lieutenants who had set himself up as a rival rebel leader.

On a quiet Sunday Elizabeth Blunt and her colleague Abubakar Sadiq of the BBC Hausa service went to its headquarters in Monrovia to interview its commander.

There was a flurry of excitement; President Doe had arrived unexpectedly.

'We went to the foot of the stairs to 'door-step' him on the way down ,' Elizabeth Blunt recalls. 'Then there was an even bigger schmozzle and some of Johnson's people arrived. Johnson started rampaging about – he was obviously quite drunk – and he kept trying to go up the stairs to where Doe was. Suddenly there was the clicking of bolts; there was a nice big old-fashioned filing cabinet, and I decided to stand by that so I could duck behind it if necessary. Then one of the Nigerians from the peace-keeping force grabbed me and told me to lie down, and someone pulled Sadiq the other way.

'Then Johnson came in, shouting and raving, and told his men to open fire. For an hour and a half I lay on the floor in the middle of a deafening gun battle. They were loosing off with everything; they even had anti-aircraft guns. A lot of it was just firing in general, but they were hunting down and killing Doe's people who weren't putting up much of a fight. Some outside tried to fire back, but a lot of them just tore off their uniforms and tried to hide. When I finally came out the whole forecourt was covered in bodies, most of them lying face down. It was like a bad Western.'

President Doe himself was wounded, captured, and taken away to be tortured to death. Johnson's soldiers videoed the gruesome scene and later offered the tape to all Western (but not African) news agencies as an example of how dictators were dealt with by a 'liberating' force.

The BBC was first with the news, even before the American State Department. A story went around Monrovia that it had been an American set-up. The Americans had been unsuccesful in their efforts to persuade Doe to leave the country so that peace could return. So, the story went, when he left his hide-out to visit the peace-keeping force they tipped off Prince Johnson.

Dorothy Grenfell Williams preparing to interview James Gichuru, of the Kenya 'African National Union', in 1960.

True? 'It's perfectly possible', is the verdict of Elizabeth Blunt.

The Liberian civil war was nicknamed 'The BBC's war' – it was not meant as a compliment – and President Doe himself once complained that he was fighting two wars – one against the international press, especially the BBC. Charles Taylor built his campaign on publicity and used the BBC to do it, according to Elizabeth Blunt, while the government side treated the media with the utmost suspicion. In a diary of events published in the BBC magazine *Focus on Africa* (named after the programme) she summarised the problem:

'Where does that leave the BBC? With a big audience, certainly, and a big responsibility. And with the accusation that it was the BBC airwaves that let the rebels get as far as they did, and with the fear that this criticism may be justified. But also with the sense that the balance has shifted. In the beginning

President Doe was known by his acts, Charles Taylor only by his words. By now, enough time has gone by for Taylor's acts to begin to speak for themselves. Now armed men on both sides are trying to find BBC reporters and kill them. I suppose I should be happy.' There is actually a happier side; there is to be a Liberian school named after her – the Liz Blunt kindergarten school.

The BBC has been broadcasting to Africa since 1940. At first it was mainly to the white population, and in English. It now broadcasts in six languages – English, French, Hausa, Portuguese, Somali and Swahili. In some countries its influence is remarkable. In Somalia, for example, it is the only source of unbiased information. During the fighting which led to the overthrow of President Siad Barre, when Mogadishu Radio was off the air, it was the only source of any information.

Officially the regular audience to the Somali Service is 41 percent of the population, but the service regards this as an under-estimate. There are various stories about its popularity. A British anthropologist travelling by bus was astonished when the driver stopped it in the middle of nowhere so that he and his passengers could hear its transmission without the noise from the engine. When a medical team from Médecins Sans Frontières went back into the capital, Mogadishu, they found people waiting for them at the general hospital; they had heard on the Somali service that they were due back.

It is not only people living in Somalia who listen; Somalis abroad do as well. The service instituted a *Missing Persons* programme to try to reunite families torn apart by the continuing civil war. About 800 letters a month came in from Somalis all over the world. Cassettes of transmissions of the regular service circulate in California.

In Cardiff, a grant from the local council enables the service to be recorded on the telephone from London and re-broadcast at the Somali community centre. Bengali, Hindi and Urdu programmes are also re-broadcast by BBC local radios in Britain for speakers of those languages living in the United Kingdom.

The African Service in English acts as a forum for debate on political subjects. Politicians are interviewed, letters from listeners, often very controversial, are read on the air; sometimes their names are omitted to protect them. The moves towards multi-party democracy are reflected in programmes, although the Head of the African Service, Dorothy Grenfell Williams, says it does not take sides.

Not everybody appreciates this activity. A listener in Tanzania wrote: '*Focus on Africa* is a source of trouble in Africa. You are creating chaos and disturbances in many African countries e.g, Kenya, Zambia, Liberia and Ethiopia to name just a few. By carrying the voice of the opponents to various governments you indirectly ask people to rebel against their governments.'

This was the view taken by President Arap Moi when in 1988 he accused the BBC of supporting subversion in his country. An 'opposition person' who had worked for the BBC was roving around seeking cause to challenge the government, he said. It so happened that the Managing Director of the World Service, John Tusa, was in Kenya at the time. He said he regretted the unwarranted attack and that any recent study of the BBC's coverage of Kenya showed it to be reasonable and balanced.

Dorothy Grenfell Williams, daughter of the first Head of the African Service, John Grenfell Williams, says dissidents are not given air-time all that often. In any case: 'We are utterly scrupulous in giving both sides exactly the same treatment and exactly the same weight.... One of our problems is that the governments which complain are very often the very same governments which are the most difficult for us to get on the air.'

A BBC Pashto poster encouraging 'Good Health' education for the family.

One part of the continent which the BBC has not been able to penetrate with much success is South Africa. The audience there is tiny – five percent of the whites and a mere 0.3 percent of the blacks.

The South African Broadcasting Corporation provides a lively service on FM and medium wave in a whole range of African languages; South Africans do not have the habit of listening on short wave. The new medium wave transmitter in Lesotho, it is hoped, will increase the audience. But broadcasting in English alone will not suffice.

Dorothy Grenfell Williams advocates a mixed Zulu/Xhosa service (the languages are mutually understandable): 'If we're really going to break through into big numbers, that's what we've got to do.'

The Pashto service to Afghans has reached big numbers in just over ten years of existence. It started in 1981 after the Soviet move into Afghanistan. According to Gordon Adam, its head, it probably has about two million regular listeners, rising to four million at times of crisis in the country itself, in the refugee camps in Pakistan and among Pashto speakers in the Gulf. Other radio stations include the name of the country – Voice of America, All-India Radio and so on – and many Afghans thought the BBC was a country; a visitor was once asked: 'How's the weather in the BBC?'

It is an example of how a small service – it broadcasts one hour a day, with additional programmes on certain days – can have a big influence because it is trusted and meets a need.

It was even reported that opposing Afghan guerrilla forces agreed a ceasefire for one hour each day so that they could listen to the Pashto service without interruption!

Afghanistan has the highest child mortality rate in the world, and because of the fighting such health services as it had have broken down. So the Pashto service has gone in for giving health advice, using short dramatic sketches. For a year these took the form of a weekly soap opera which won a Sony radio award for outstanding service to the community, the only time such an award has gone to a foreign language radio programme. The programmes receive funding from United Nations agencies, and deal with such matters as coping with disability, nutrition, immunisation, heroin addiction and advising farmers on pests.

They have an impact. A series on the dangers of unexploded mines had Afghan boys in refugee camps playing 'BBC mines games.'

And when two health workers in the east of the country wrote to the BBC they had a pleasant surprise. They had been organising tetanus inoculations, and complained that men came and brought their children but not their wives, although it was very important that they too should be inoculated because of possible complications in childbirth. By chance the Pashto service broadcast a short sketch emphasising the importance of inoculation to women; over the next few days three hundred women turned up.

The title of this book is taken in part from a letter from a Burmese listener who found in the BBC a sense of freedom impossible in his own country. The Burmese service was one of those threatened with abolition in 1981 but was eventually reprieved. In 1989 it received 98,000 letters, the highest of any service in Bush House. The government of Burma had published a book a year before called *Skyful of Lies*, to rebut what it described as the 'disinformation' broadcast by the BBC and the Voice of America.

Reply to BBC broadcast about recovery of peace in Rangoon

29-8-88, 8:15 pm BBC broadcast. This was a report about recovery of peace in Rangoon. The report said: "As huge, whole demonstrations went on in Rangoon, a group of influential ex-politicians has formed a body to restore peace and maintain essential public service. Christopher Gunness has reported that riots have broken out in prisons throughout the country. Hundred and thousands of demonstrators had gathered in Rangoon and shouted anti-government slogans and demands for removal of current leadership. A diplomat has however said that Rangoon appeared to have regained peace after a week-end of anarchy."

Here we would like to point out that we do not understand what he meant by saying a committee has been formed. We do not know which organisation he meant: He did not mention the name either or who were in it. We find that it was therefore only an advice to form such a body.

Then Christopher Gunness was also said to have reported that official sources had said the whole country was in panic. Which was the official source? Who was he? Which department? From where? When was it received? N...

is known to have been formed for the purpose of restoration of peace in the whole country and of maintaining essential public services.

Here I find that the Constitution allowed only one party and emergence of another parallel party was illegal. It was only an emergency body formed during the emergency. But this the BBC had broadcast for the whole country to know. The terms of reference stated by BBC was surprising. They have no authority that they may restore peace. Yet the term was used to mislead the people. We can guess a lot as to what its objectives were. The BBC spotlighted it to promote the anti-government protests.

Now I will discuss the BBC's press review. The review said: "Neil Kelly reporting in the *Times* said the release of prisoners was an attempt to escalate disturbances and a ploy by Dr Maung Maung to demonstrate that a strong government was needed in the country. Neil Kelly has also reported that hundreds of Party officials have quite their posts in the whole country and monks and students have taken over their responsibilities. This was because demonstrations have been taken over by lawless and

Part of a page from 'A Skyful of Lies', a book compiled by the Burmese government in 1988.

125

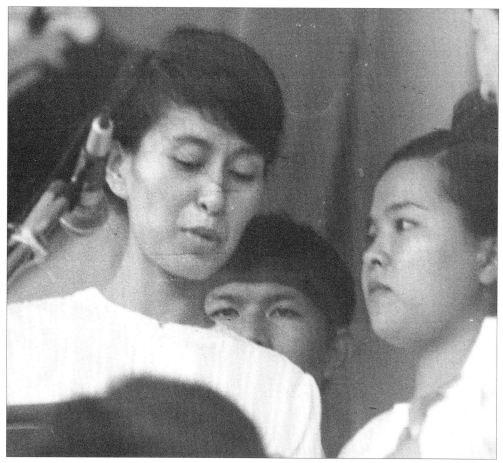

The 1991 Nobel Peace Prize was awarded to the detained opposition leader, Aung San Suu Kyi, for her non-violent protests in the cause of human rights in Burma, one of the most isolated regimes in the world.

This curious work consists of transcripts of broadcasts during August 1988, a time of unrest, followed by detailed replies to them. It is especially critical of the BBC. 'That the BBC is particularly trying to subvert Burma is especially clear,' says the anonymous author...' The BBC has nurtured a spoil (sic) of opposition to Burma. The ill-will perpetrated by the BBC to Burma has grown as high as the Himalaya mountains.'

Like the rest of Bush House, the Burmese Service is trying to attract more women listeners and, in November 1991, launched a series of special programmes for women.

A Burmese government commentator complained: 'Not content with interfering in our internal affairs, the BBC is now meddling in the kitchen.' The series included a two-part documentary on Aung San Suu Kyi, who had just won the Nobel Peace Prize. She is leader of the National League for Democracy, and was put under house arrest in 1989. In the following year her party won a landslide election victory; the hardline military regime simply ignored the result and continued in power.

Six months before the election some American embassy staff visited villages in Upper Burma to try to find out how the people there would vote. The answer they received from a number of them was: 'We shall wait until we get the advice of the BBC before we decide.' The BBC does not, of course give advice of this sort. 'We were very

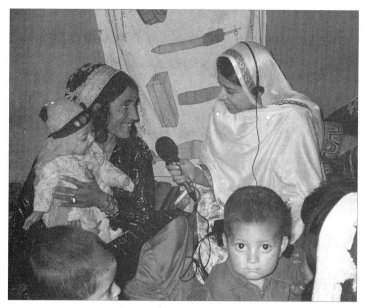

Sasia Haleem, of the Pashto sevice, interviewing a woman in a refugee camp in Pakistan in 1991.

careful to give fair coverage to the election,' says the Head of the Burmese Service, Derek Brooke-Wavell. 'The closest we came to giving advice was to say it looked as if it was going to be a two-horse race between the National League for Democracy and the government (National Unity Party).'

Burma is largely isolated from the world, and information about conditions there is difficult to come by. Letters from listeners help to fill in the inevitable gaps in knowledge. One of them showed the dictatorial nature of the regime but leavened the horror with wry humour.

He said the BBC had 'truthfully and clearly' broadcast that the responsibility for Aung San Suu Kyi being stripped of membership of her party (in December 1991) lay at the door of the regime. (It had threatened the leaders still at large that the party would be banned if they did not do so.) Since then soldiers had been going around in his town confiscating radio sets and fining people who had listened to the BBC: 'People are now afraid to listen to you openly. Can't you broadcast the false news so that we can tune into you fearlessly?'

Finally, an example of a different type of impact. Douglas Kennedy, writing in the *Daily Mail* early in 1992, described how he gave a lift to an 'elderly Aboriginal gentle-man' in the Western Australian bush. 'He began to bombard me with questions about life in Britain. Did I approve of John Major? Was this Gascoigne fellow everything he was cracked up to be? And did Alan Ayckbourn have a new play in the West End?'

Douglas Kennedy went on: 'I was a little stunned to learn that this man – who later told me he had never ventured out of the West Australian bush – actually knew a thing or two about one of Britain's leading contemporary playwrights. As it turned out, he'd heard a few Ayckbourn plays on the BBC World Service and, thanks to such World Service arts programmes as *Meridian*, he also happened to be very up to date with the state of British drama.'

CHAPTER THIRTEEN

The Fall of Communism: Part I

A LISTENER IN ROMANIA spoke for many when he wrote to the BBC early in 1990: 'I cannot find words to thank you for everything you have done for this country ever since 1944, but especially during the last two months.'

It was the liberation of Europe all over again, forty-five years later. The collapse of communism was the most significant – and breathtaking – event in the second half of the twentieth century. Its implications are still unclear. With the old Cold War certainties gone, nobody can foretell how a Europe without communism will develop. We are all trying to look ahead into the mist.

International broadcasting played its part in the collapse From the beginning of the Cold War Western radio stations, known collectively to some Russians as 'The Voices', beamed their messages to those living under communism. Their message was similar, but their tones were different. The two American stations, Radio Free Europe (for the satellite countries) and Radio Liberty (for the Soviet Union) set themselves up as alternative home services.

They concentrated on events of immediate concern to their audiences and were on the air throughout the day and, in the case of Radio Liberty, throughout the night as well. They secured the largest audience of all Western radios. The Voice of America came second in the number of hours broadcast (and size of audience) to most East European countries, with the BBC third.

A senior member of Radio Free Europe (William A. Buell) once divided Western radios into 'hard sell' and 'soft sell', the first believing that broadcasting is an instrument of political and social change to be used aggressively, the second that it should be used in an objective and balanced way, leaving the listeners to make their own judgements. His own station and Voice of America leaned towards the hard sell in their early days, but have since modified their attitudes. The BBC has been soft sell consistently and has been at times criticised by Russian exiles for its 'wishy-washy' approach.

But there is rather more to it than that. Peter Fraenkel, former Controller of European Services has argued: 'It is not that we do not recognise absolute values of right and wrong, but that we have considerable diffidence about pressing our values upon others. The attitude 'on the one hand, on the other' is a reflection both of a pluralistic society and of a respect for our listeners. 'Give them the facts,'we have always argued: 'Give them the arguments on either side. Let them make up their own minds." (*Western Broadcasting over the Iron Curtain*, edited by K.R.M. Short, Croom and Helm, 1986).

Something of the same attitude was expressed by Alexander Lieven, then Head of the East European Service when, in 1971, he urged a 'cool, detached, almost clinical' approach. His point was that people living under communism did not need to be told that it was discredited; they knew that from their daily lives. Their own media had made them sceptical of all sources of information; they wanted accurate news of the outside world. 'We should not' he wrote, 'adopt an automatically hostile attitude... and at all costs abstain from pettiness, pinpricks, rubbing salt into the wounds, sarcasm, polemics or superior "holier than thou" or "you are always wrong" attitudes.'

Another aspect of this approach was the argument that the BBC needed to continue to broadcast to countries in Western as well as Eastern Europe so that it was not seen as just an anti-communist propaganda outfit. It should speak with one voice to all. In the words of Peter Fraenkel: 'It does seem to me essential for the reputation of the BBC – and for the personal intergrity of its staff – to speak with the same voice of torture in Spain or Greece or Latin America as in the Soviet Union, while not losing sight of the scale of repression.'

Surveys carried out at the time among people from communist countries travelling to or living in the West showed there was a considerable audience for Western broadcasts. What influence did they have? For the BBC, 'it's not quantifiable,' says Barry Elliott, head of the Central European Service. 'In terms of keeping hope alive and spreading democratic ideas, of really putting it to people that there were alternatives, yes, I think we did have a role. We were not propounding a change of regime – that wasn't part of our job – but we were stimulating the democratic process and providing a whole range of views, and by reporting strikes and demonstrations that people would not have heard about from their own media we encouraged them to come out and demonstrate.'

An early sign of the coming collapse was reported by the Hungarian service in 1987. The Hungarian Writers Union threw out its communist leadership and elected one which included non-communists. Klara Whitthall, Deputy Head of the Hungarian Section, described what happened: 'Nick Thorpe (the section's stringer) sent us a report which we decided to broadcast. This was a hush-hush affair because it couldn't get out that a communist-led organisation like the Writers' Union had problems with its management. When we broadcast it complaints came in through party channels. At that time Nick Thorpe needed an extension to his visa, and the party threatened they wouldn't allow him to stay on because of this but eventually it was smoothed over. That was the first time the party reacted to our programmes so sharply. We used to have gentle complaints from the Hungarian Embassy in London, but this was the first time the party felt vulnerable enough to complain to us – in no uncertain terms.'

The authorities also objected to coverage of a widespread protest movement against building a new Danube dam and hydro-electric power station. Reports of this nature undermine the credibility of the authorities who try to suppress them and, in the words of European Controller, Andrew Taussig, have 'a sapping effect.'

The Head of the Hungarian Section, Peter Szente, remembers listening to the BBC when he was a very young child, during the last war: 'I remember my grandparents having to close the windows even on a very hot day so that neighbours wouldn't hear us listening.' Listening continued during the early years of communism: 'The day Churchill was re-elected after the defeat of the Labour government (1951) – we heard about it on the BBC – my uncle got out the only bottle of decent champagne we had left from before the war. He broke it open because now that Churchill was back, he said, the Tommies would be coming to liberate us.'

Peter Szente escaped to England after taking part in the 1956 uprising. Not at that time speaking any English, he spent years doing dead-end jobs – including being a kitchen porter at a London hotel – before discovering that he could get a grant to go to university: 'In Hungary we were told that in the West you had to pay to go to university,' he explained. He joined the BBC in 1974.

In Hungary, he says, it was axiomatic, even among people who never listened to the BBC, that other stations might be first with the news 'but with the BBC you can rely on what you hear.' In 1991 he and Klara Whittall went to Budapest to publicise the news that Hungarian state radio was going to transmit one of their section's programmes on FM. They devised a questionnaire to find out how people viewed their service. There were 1448 replies. Of these 15% said they never listened to it. But 100% described it as objective, impartial, unbiased and so on, including those who said they never listened. That, he says, is its brand image.

'It is not only its image among the intellectuals who do listen, but in a much wider sphere,' Peter Szente adds. 'Here is a minor example: when I ring and say I want to book a restaurant table and they say it's absolutely impossible, the place is full, I say it's the BBC. I get a table.'

Poland was one communist country where it was possible to listen to the BBC

without fear of persecution by the police, and it has always had a substantial audience. It was subject to ritual denunciations from time to time, but perhaps they were not meant to be taken too seriously. Konrad Syrop was head of the Central European Service for a time in the early seventies and visited Poland. 'I had a session with the head of the Polish radio foreign service, a member of the Central Committee and a dyed-in-the-wool Stalinist,' he recalls. 'We went at each other quite angrily for about two hours. He was accusing me of interference in Poland's internal affairs, and I was asking him for examples. The few he gave me were entirely justified as news items. When the talking was over it was lunchtime, and he drove me to a very expensive restaurant. Vodka was flowing, and he mellowed considerably. He drove me back to my hotel, and when he left me he said: "You speak Polish, so you won't get lost. We've got the latest gadgets from the Americans, so we won't lose you. Have a good time."'

The Polish Service was the first in East and Central Europe to interview people by telephone – in 1976 – according to the Head of the section, Eugeniusz (Gienek) Smolar. That was a year in which there were protests against price-rises and a workers' defence committee – forerunner of Solidarity – was formed. 'We learned to trust their information about violations of human and civil rights,' he says. 'The communist authorities denied the violations, and we tried very hard to get their reactions but had to say they refused to comment or quote the newspapers. The authorities finally realised they were getting a raw deal so by the end of the seventies they had started giving occasional interviews.'

The crackdown on Solidarity and imposition of martial law in December 1981 were what Gienek Smolar described as 'the moment of truth' for the Polish Service. The military government closed the telephone

In Gdansk, Poland, people gather in front of the Sports Centre in June, 1981, at Solidarity's national convention.

networks and cut telex lines. The service asked its 'friends' all over the world for help by interviewing people who had just arrived from Poland. All the information was sifted in London. There were other sources too – the Foreign Office and its equivalents in other Western capitals.

And there was one route for information which has not been publicly revealed until now, ten years later. The computer line in the Department of Mathematics of the Polish Academy of Sciences remained open to the Mathematical Centre in Vienna. Students and young academics used it to put over information for the exclusive use of the BBC Polish Service.

1981 also saw the renewal of jamming, not just by the local authorities but by the Soviet Union as well. The military government frequently denounced the BBC; there was on average a strong protest to the British Embassy every two weeks. The service

maintained its principle of being right rather than first with the news. For example, there was a report that Tadeusz Mazowiecki, who was later to become the first Solidarity Prime Minister, had died in a prison camp; there was even a mass for his soul at Nôtre Dame cathedral in Paris. 'We came to the conclusion that the news could not be verified,' recalled Gienek Smolar. 'He was too prominent a figure just to be killed by a policeman and a confidential source in the Vatican couldn't confirm it. So we were the only broadcaster in Polish not to broadcast the news; I think that was a victory for sound journalism.'

With Mikhail Gorbachev's accession to power in 1985 the situation began gradually to ease. The Polish service was able to approach government officials for interviews, at the same time requesting an end to the jamming. Something of a breakthrough came that year with a report claiming the prison

Berlin, 1990. A young East German brandishes a first edition whose headline reads 'It's done! The wall is open.'

authorities had been torturing inmates. A member of the service telephoned the head of the prison department at the Ministry of Justice, and he agreed to an interview – the first since the declaration of martial law. Jamming was finally lifted in 1988.

Gienek Smolar says the service helped to bring government and opposition together in the 'round table' discussions of 1988-89 which led to the establishment of democracy in Poland. 'At first they couldn't talk to each other in the same room, but they could through the BBC,' he says. 'We probably helped them to understand each other better. Being the BBC and not antagonistic to either side we facilitated communication, and the arguments that were finally put on the table were actually the subjects that had been for discussion on the BBC Polish service.'

It was Tadeusz Mazowiecki, once reported dead, who had an idea which was to be taken up enthusiastically by the World Service. Discussing the future of Polish broadcasting in 1989, he suggested that the BBC should be involved in training. The upshot was a course in London for 36 broadcasters, to be followed later by broadcasters from Hungary and Czechoslovakia. The money was provided by the British government's Knowhow Fund.

Audience research in October 1991 showed that the BBC had become the most popular foreign broadcaster in Poland. It had a regular audience of 8.7% of the population, compared to 7.9% for VOA and 7.5% for RFE. Most of the listening was on FM.

The Polish service was being re-broadcast from satellite on 17 local stations and two private ones, covering 95% of the population. It used to be transmitted nationally by the Polish state radio on medium wave, but that slot was bought by RFE, an example of one of the snags of re-broadcasting. All the same, re-broadcasting has continued to grow in former countries of the Soviet bloc, including what was East Germany.

In Czechoslovakia, where listening to the BBC under communism was more difficult than it was in Poland, a 24-hour service began in December 1990 in three cities, Prague, Bratislava and Brno. They transmit programmes in Czech, Slovak and English, as well as English-language lessons.

And in Sofia the BBC acquired an FM transmitter which broadcasts its programmes to a potential audience of three-and-a-half million people.

Re-broadcasting helps to ensure that the BBC can continue to speak in their own language to people who have only recently thrown off communism. It is a voice made familar to them under a system which tried to control their thoughts, and it may well help them in the difficult transition towards democracy.

CHAPTER FOURTEEN

The Fall of Communism: Part II

A STORY which the BBC broke to the world was the persecution of the Turkish minority in Bulgaria; it led to the downfall of the Bulgarian leader, Todor Zhivkov, after more than 35 years in power and was unusual in that the original information came on the telephone from the people affected. In 1986 the Bulgarian and Turkish Services began phone-ins. The Bulgarian Service wanted people to telephone their requests for the pop programme; mail deliveries were erratic and liable to be censored. But, as well as making their requests, callers began to make comments on reception and the contents of the programmes.

The Turkish section head, Zeki Okar, takes up the story: 'In early May 1989 we began to get calls from Bulgarian Turks, telling us in hushed voices that there had been massacres here and there. Then news of the deportation of ringleaders started to come in. After careful checking we started to run the story; we were able to get hold of some of the people who had been deported in Vienna. We were the only organisation to report the story for about three days. Even the Prime Minister of Turkey said that all he knew about it was what he had heard on the BBC.' The story made banner headlines in every Turkish newspaper – quoting the BBC – and the Foreign Ministry asked Bush House for any further information.

There were calls to the Bulgarian Service as well, starting in March. 'How long will the assassination go on for?' asked one caller rhetorically. 'Our plight gets worse every day.' By May there was news of demonstrations and a hunger strike. There was also an indication of organisation behind the protests: 'We started this campaign in order to publicise the cruel assimilation of the Turkish and other minorities in Bulgaria, both in Europe and around the world. At this moment we need help, and that is to have our names and villages broadcast. You will receive this information regularly, and we would like it to be passed to the Turkish section too...'

A handful of callers objected to the fact that the Bulgarian Service was reporting the protests. An anonymous woman from Sofia, calling, she said, on behalf of a group of colleagues, complained: 'Stop being so preoccupied with our country and our people. To use a Bulgarian proverb – don't weep over other people's graves....Besides, we know that England, too, is getting rid of its Turkish population....Mrs Thatcher is personally throwing them out.'

The story unearthed by the BBC had momentous consequences. Police fired on a Turkish demonstration and dozens of people were killed. As the BBC central Europe correspondent Misha Glenny put it, this provoked a diplomatic crisis with Ankara and a potentially explosive situation within Bulgaria itself: 'Too late Zhivkov recognised his mistake and attempted to cut his losses by suddenly giving Bulgarian Turks a passport and allowing them to emigrate to Turkey. The exodus soon developed into the biggest movement of peoples in modern Europe.' (*The Rebirth of History*, by Misha Glenny, Penguin Books, 1990). The whole affair, says Misha Glenny, was 'a dreadful miscalculation'. It resulted in the ousting of the unpopular Todor Zhivkov in a 'palace revolution' supported by the Soviet Union.

Another country, another revolution. 'We like to think we were the first with the news about the events in Timisoara,' says the deputy head of the Romanian section, Mrs Obreja. This, of course, was where the Romanian revolution started in December 1989 – although it is now referred to as 'The Events' rather than the revolution since there is a suggestion that Ceausescu's colleagues had been already planning to topple him and took advantage of the unrest. 'We got wind of what was happening through a stringer in Budapest who had relatives in Timisoara,' says Mrs Obreja. 'We reported the demonstrations, the army coming in and the shooting.'

A few days later the Bush House diplomatic correspondent, Mark Brayne, travelled adventurously to Bucharest. He flew first to Belgrade via Munich, then hired a taxi (which was to cost him $1,850). 'We filled up with food and mineral water because we had heard rumours that the Securitate had poisoned the water supply,' he said later. He reached the Romanian border at about one in the morning, found the border guards nervous but friendly enough and after about an hour was able to persuade them to let him in. 'About ten kilometres inside the border an army jeep overtook us and flagged us down. The driver was terrified; he thought we were going to be shot. An army officer got in the taxi and said they had received orders from Bucharest for us to leave and we drove back to the border. Luckily he could speak English, and I sweet-talked him, to persuade him to try and get permission for us. He said he would see what he could do. Finally, at about three o'clock we were told we could go, so we drove through what was left of the night and arrived in Bucharest about dawn.'

Shooting was still going on, and they were unable to reach the Intercontinental Hotel, which was in an area that had been sealed off. Instead they went to another hotel where the management arranged for an open telephone line to London and rigged him up a makeshift studio, putting mattresses on the walls to deaden the sound. Mark Brayne says this was the most exciting story in his career. In three weeks he filed 75 news despatches and innumerable interviews. He had a bad moment when troops saw him speaking into a microphone, and he thought they had mistaken him for a member of the Securitate. A particularly moving moment came at Christmas when, for the first time since the Communists took power, church bells rang out and people sang carols which he recorded and played over to London for the whole world to hear.

In London all 14 members of the Romanian section voluntarily gave up their Christmas leave. A senior programme assistant flew to Bulgaria, crossed into Romania by train, then hitchhiked to Bucharest and began filing stories. Staff at Bucharest Radio recorded a message thanking the section for years of 'accurate

In Bucharest on Christmas Day, 1989, after the fall of the Ceaucescu government. A Romanian tank driver distributes free newspapers: for many citizens it was the first opportunity ever to read a free press.

reporting and information' about their country.

A listener in Timisoara wrote just over two months later: 'I have been listening to you for about 50 years, and this was a way for me to survive. To-day we need you even more in order for a new generation to learn that they have a chance of a better life.' And from Moldavia came a tribute which conjures up an unusual picture: 'I have persistently listened to your broadcasts, many times hidden under a blanket in my monastic cell...I am convinced you made an important contribution to what we Romanians are experiencing to-day.'

The Romanian service has a substantial audience still, but its credibility was damaged by a mistake made on BBC TV news in the autumn of 1990. Pictures of a demonstration in Sofia, with a building in flames, were wrongly described as showing Bucharest. The Romanian government, concerned at the influence of the BBC, seized on the error. 'It was like a godsend to them,' says Mrs Obreja. 'They used it in a very perverse way to undermine our credibility. No matter how many apologies and explanations we made they used it as a propaganda tool to hit us on the head.' For many years Romania was a country closed to the BBC ; after 'the events' the service set up a permanent presence there, producers taking it in turns. Other services to East and Central Europe did the same.

In what was the Soviet Union listeners showed what the head of the Russian service, David Morton, describes as 'a dedication unparalleled.' Some people, he says, spent whole evenings listening to foreign broadcasts – not just the BBC but also Radio Liberty, Voice of America and Deutsche Welle.

With glasnost and the end of jamming the Russian service was able to reorganise its programmes, cutting the number of repeats and, among other things, introducing a new discussion programme. It had a moment of fame when Mrs Thatcher took part in a phone-in in July 1988. 'By the time the broadcast started there were very few calls,' David Morton said. 'But once we were on the air and she started speaking there was an overwhelming response – the switchboard just went mad. I think they didn't really believe the Prime Minister would talk to the Russian Service until they heard it.'

Before the changes in the Soviet Union it was estimated that about 16 million people

Listening to the news in Moscow on a portable radio. An eight-man junta had just staged a coup in August 1991 to overthrow President Gorbachev. The coup collapsed after three days.

listened to the Russian service at least once a week. Glassnost provides a challenge, since the domestic media are, of course, much freer and more numerous than they were. There is less need now to listen to 'The Voices'. The following extracts from an interview conducted in March 1990 with a young electronics engineer suggests that the BBC has nevertheless won the loyalty of at least some of its listeners.

'I like to listen to the BBC because firstly I have found through the BBC a completely separate world for myself through the radio, a world which I could never know existed while I was living here, in my country... I would go to bed late usually since it was at the time when I was studying at the Institute and at that late time I would normally listen to all the news coverage and the later programmes, then they would start the jazz and music programmes of course, so all that somehow subconsciously would eat into my mind and would to some degree determine my outlook, my attitude to things...

'Now I think my outlook, my ideas about the world, are more or less complete and I can only be thankful to the BBC in particular, well, perhaps some others, but the BBC mostly.... But I am really grateful for the programmes I was listening to because they helped me to form my own opinions about the world, my attitude to controversial things. It was, so to speak, my source, the one I could rely on, it was a source of self-education for me.'

Asked about the listening habits of other people, he said: 'It is easier for me to talk about the people of my age, since from my daily conversations with my friends, those who graduated from the Institute with me or even those I went to school with or those I work with, I know that all of them are listening to the BBC; at any rate I don't know anybody who doesn't listen to that station.

And when he was asked if he thought the

'They're queueing for bread and we're queueing to be interviewed by the BBC'

A chance to speak into a BBC microphone was a sure crowd-puller in beleaguered Moscow…

…And this was one of the men to whom they wished to speak; Tim Whewell, of the BBC.

Russian service should continue, he was emphatic: 'I just can't imagine myself without the Russian service of the BBC, since I have liked this station for so many years and if it loses its Russian service then I just won't be able to understand the English broadcasts and for me it will be something like – well, some window that has been shut, something that was always trustworthy and stable. I could always, when I would come home, switch the set on, find this station and just relax while listening. And if something like that happens, then it would be some-thing irreparable. I would have to take some very radical steps to compensate for such enormous damage. But then I believe your question was only a rhetorical one.'

This interview was one of many conduct-ed for a publicity video. But, allowing for that, it remains a remarkable piece of evidence for the impact of the Russian service on intelligent young people. As for older people, there is more to say about Mikhail Gorbachev and the attempted coup

in 1991. At the news conference at which he said he heard the BBC best of all, there was apparently no BBC correspondent. 'Never mind,' he said with a smile. 'The BBC knows everything already.'

In fact, during the coup two World Service correspondents, Tim Whewell for the news department and Grigory Nekhroshev for the Russian Service, reported direct from the White House from where Boris Yeltsin was leading the resistance. Tim Whewell found an abandoned office there, put through a call to the BBC Moscow Office and organised a telephone link with London. International calls from the White House were being blocked, but this counted as a local call and stayed open.

Elizabeth Smith, Controller of English Services, has this story to tell: 'When Gorbachev was leaving the Soviet Parliament a few days after his return to Moscow, he waved the press away. But Grigory Nekhroshev called out that he was from the BBC Russian service. Gorbachev stopped and said hello and shook his hand warmly. The BBC had been his main source of information during the confinement, he said. Its reports had been the most reliable and thorough and had confirmed what he had thought from the outset; the whole action was a conspiracy and the military takeover doomed to failure.

He should now be able to hear it still more clearly. In October 1991 an agreement was signed for Radio Russia to broadcast two half-hour BBC Russian Service current-affairs programmes each weekend. They were to be beamed by satellite and then rebroadcast all over the Russian Federation, which stretches from St. Petersburg to Vladivostok.

The impending dissolution of the Soviet Union led to a decision to add Ukrainian to the languages transmitted. The BBC had been arguing the case for a long time for both Ukrainian and Uzbek, the latter to reach the largest single population group in Soviet Central Asia. With Ukraine declaring itself independent, there was little point in expecting its people to listen to broadcasts in Russian. As David Morton put it: 'In some instances, not all, you should be thinking about broadcasting in other languages because the risk is that if you don't, you won't be acceptable to them – and if you're not acceptable you might as well give up broadcasting.' In October 1991 the FCO saw the logic so far as Ukrainian was concerned and it was planned to start transmissions of up to seven hours early in 1992.

Yugoslavia provided another example of how the changes in Eastern Europe are affecting the languages the BBC uses. For many years it spoke to the country in Slovene and Serbo-Croat. With the fighting between Serbs and Croats in 1991 Serbo-Croat, imposed under Tito, became unacceptable in Croatia. The BBC was already being re-broadcast in Slovenia; if it wished Croatia to follow suit it had to broadcast in Croatian, not all that different,

but not sounding like Serbian. The Foreign Office demurred; it would look like an official British recognition that the country had split and the Yugoslavia Federation was no more. Finally broadcasting reasons overcame diplomatic ones, and the change was sanctioned.

The collapse of communism was not, of course, repeated in China, in spite of mass demonstrations by students and others. Until the opening of the Hong Kong transmitter in 1987 it was difficult to hear the BBC in large parts of China, and its audience was well below that of Voice of America. Better reception and in particular its reporting of the events in Tianenmen Square have now given it a mass audience. No audience research has been possible in China, but the head of the Chinese Section, Elizabeth Wright, estimates it at tens of millions. Its broadcasting hours trebled between 1987 and 1991, but were still only 3 hours a day in Mandarin and three-quarters of an hour in Cantonese, compared with the eight hours a day of VOA.

Mark Brayne, who had been the BBC correspondent in Beijing, was back there in May 1989 to report the visit of Mr Gorbachev. He witnessed the demonstrations which, as they grew, he described in a despatch as 'the most fundamental challenge in 40 years to China's communist leadership.' Mark Brayne also witnessed the first moves into Beijing by the army, stopped by makeshift barricades erected by the ordinary people of Beijing. 'The power of radio was quite extraordinary,' he said. 'You could just drop into a shop or a block of flats, find one of the communal telephones the Chinese have, ring the international exchange and ask for a reversed charge call to London. I knew all the ladies on the exchange, and they were all very friendly, so I was able to get through in no time at all.'

He once telephoned from a hut used as a

coal bunker. On another occasion, just after martial law had been declared, he was using a telephone in a shop when officials came in and cut him off in the middle of an interview.

Mark Brayne left China before the massacre, in common with a number of other journalists. Although the hardliners at the top had won, it seemed as if the army, having been humiliated by people power, was set on avoiding any further confrontation. Many of the demonstrators from outside Beijing had returned home and things seemed to be winding down. But the army was to return in force.

Simon Long, who was a stringer for Bush House at the time (and stayed on for another two years) recalls how the students used to urge him: 'Tell the world'. This, of course, was what he and his colleagues were doing, but he was also telling the Chinese people. Loudspeakers on university campuses and wallposters reproduced BBC reports. When troops, tanks and armoured personnel carriers moved into Tianenmen Square to crush the demonstrations he was locked in a hotel nearby but was able to watch at least part of the shooting.

June 4 1989 was a Sunday, and the Chinese Service was due to broadcast a programme of short stories after the news. Some members of the staff were on holiday and impossible to reach, and there were only two actually on duty.

Mary Wang, assistant head of the service, recalls that day: 'I was at home and when I saw the first flash on television I rushed to the office. We managed to get a recording of what Kate Adie had reported and translate it just in time for our morning transmission. Then the three of us put together a half-hour programme for the evening. We telephoned a Chinese-speaking Yugoslav journalist in Beijing, and we telephoned a hospital. A doctor said there were 26 bodies there, and the corridor was full of wounded. He said they were having to turn people away – and

a lot of them were going to die – and doctors were weeping as they did their work. We broadcast his account in his own words. This was important because the Chinese authorities said no-one was killed.'

Western estimates of the numbers killed that night vary between 700 and 3,000, but the Chinese government started what Elizabeth Wright has described as 'one of the most complete disinformation campaigns in the history of the Chinese Communist party. With breathtaking cynicism they had clearly decided that if they were going to lie it might as well be a colossal lie.

Doctoring news footage of the events of 4 June they initially announced that only a handful of civilians had been killed in the square (and those by accident) whilst, on the contrary, armed protesters had murdered some one thousand or so innocent and heroic soldiers.' (*The Chinese People Stand Up*, by Elizabeth Wright, BBC Books, 1989).

This had some effect. A dissatisfied listener wrote to London: 'Listening to the BBC and the VOA about recent incidents that happened in China, at first I believed what you had reported. But later, when I watched CCTV's truth about students rioting in Beijing, I couldn't help blame you – the BBC – why are you spreading rumours? Damn you! I wish your company bankrupt. I wish for you all to go to hell!'

Other listeners were not taken in. 'A news blockade has been started by our government,' wrote one. 'The BBC has become the only station to give us news that ' can be trusted.' And from another: 'During the students' movements your objective reports on Tianenmen Square have given us an instant understanding of what has happened in Beijing. We're listening to you every day.'

One, who signed him or her self Super Listener, gave 'my salute to those journalists who work under such dangerous conditions. We are very grateful for reports on China,

Tensions in China, and the confrontations in Tianenmen Square in 1989, are recorded by BBC world service diplomatic correspondent Mark Brayne, here seen interviewing students in Beijing.

especially for the student seeking freedom movements. You'll go down in our history. We'll remember you for ever.'

Simon Long himself received a particularly appreciative letter. One of the odd things about this episode is that, although the Chinese authorities began jamming the Mandarin broadcasts in 1989, they did not publicly complain about the BBC.

Privately, says Simon Long, they said it was objective but made some mistakes. The first time the BBC and Voice of America were attacked was in June, 1991, for a report about a small protest at Beijing University on the second anniversary of the Tianenmen Square massacre.

Although listening fell off after the massacre, it picked up again at the time of the Gulf War. People, says Simon Long, were excited by the news and supported the US-led coalition. It was a disguised form of dissent.

141

CHAPTER FIFTEEN

Wars of the Eighties

IN FACT, the audience for the World Service increased dramatically from the very beginning of the Gulf crisis, when Iraq invaded Kuwait in August 1990. The hours of the Arabic service were immediately increased, from nine a day to ten, then ten-and-a half, rising temporarily to 14 during the fighting. The Iraqi authorities began to jam the service but gave up after about six weeks.

Soon after the invasion the BBC carried out some audience surveys in the United Arab Emirates and Cairo and Alexandria in Egypt. These showed that the number of people listening at least once a week had more than doubled – to just over the half the adult population in the UAE and just under half in Cairo and Alexandria. Later, in November, a survey of 400 adults in Amman, Jordan, suggested that one in four adults there were listening to the BBC on any given day.

Of course, not everybody liked what they were hearing. As we saw earlier, there were a number of complaints from Arab governments in the allied coalition about the alleged pro-Iraqi bias of the Arabic service. Sam Younger, Head of the Arabic Service at the time, argues that there were several reasons for this. In the early days of the crisis, before they were assured of American support, the Saudis and others were very worried and desperately sensitive to what was being said. Then there are many Jordanians and Palestinians working for the Arabic service. 'When they heard a Jordanian or Palestinian voice there was a feeling that these people must be reflecting Jordanian or Palestinian views which, of course, were pro-Iraq. And every time we interviewed a Jordanian or quoted Saddam Hussein, particu-larly in his own voice, it was assumed to show BBC support for the Iraqi side.'

There were complaints, too, from people who supported Saddam Hussein, but these were not conveyed through official channels but by letters and articles like this one from a newspaper in Jordan: 'The BBC continued... presenting and repeating the one-sided news, interviews and analyses in a style made famous by the Nazi minister of propaganda. The BBC did not only use its Arabic Service to wage war on Iraq, it also made its war-mongering the religion of all its other sections broadcasting in all the world's languages.'

Sam Younger says most of the complaints were too vague to be traced. 'When they were specific I investigated them exhaustively and none of them gave any ammunition to any accusation of serious imbalance..' In addition an independent Arabic speaker was engaged to listen to the output for six hours a week at random, and he reported on it favourably. The fact is, of course, that the Arab governments which complained did not themselves possess an independent broadcasting organisation which followed an even-handed approach; their own were state-controlled.

The 50 or so Arab broadcasters were often under severe emotional pressure. The largest single nationality represented is Egyptian, and there were fierce arguments about the justice of the allied cause. But, Sam Younger says, 'There was no instance where a member of the service did anything but keep their eye on the fact that their first priority was a journalistic one. That is why a lot of them, came to the BBC in the first place, in order to be able to operate like that.'

On the night the allied bombing began, 16/17 January 1991, one of the newsreaders was a woman who came from Iraq; her mother and sister were there. 'Imagine how someone like that felt when news came in that allied planes were bombing Baghdad. But she had to steady her nerves and read the news bulletin in a straight and unemotional way.'

Several other language services were involved in speaking to an audience in the Middle East: the Urdu and Bengali services to Pakistanis and Bangladeshis in the Gulf states, including Kuwait, for example. There were one hundred and fifty thousand Thais in Saudi Arabia and Kuwait, a hundred thousand Indonesians and fifty thousand Vietnamese. With few of them able to speak Arabic or English, they depended heavily on the BBC which put on extra transmissions in their languages. One group of Thais set off by car to escape from Kuwait to Saudi Arabia. They found the going difficult and were on the point of turning back. Then

they tuned into the BBC, heard an interview with some Thais who had succeeded in escaping, continued their journey and got out safely. The government of Thailand thanked the BBC for the help it gave to Thai nationals.

From a Tamil came a particularly grateful letter: 'When you told us about the escape route, that people were fleeing to Jordan, we took courage from it and made a dash for it. You saved our lives. We are grateful to the BBC.' People who returned safely to their own countries were also grateful. An organisation caring for those repatriated to Bangladesh, for example, said many were helped to escape by reports in the Bengali service.

The World Service in English initiated a *Gulf Link* programme for relatives to broadcast messages to English speakers trapped in Kuwait or Iraq after the invasion. 'We set it up in 24 hours,' recalls Genevieve Eckenstein, Head of Topical Tapes. 'We had some special telephone lines put in, and the moment the number was released they never stopped ringing.' Callers were offered the choice of recording their own messages or having them read on the air.

There was so much demand that the service was extended from 15 minutes on five days a week to 30 and finally 45 minutes every day. In the three months it lasted – from September to December – it transmitted six thousand messages. They included a proposal of marriage, the acceptance of a separate proposal, news of births, deaths and other family events. For the people cut off from their families, unable to receive letters or telephone calls, they were a lifeline.

A Briton back at home after being held in Iraq wrote in December: 'One of the few institutions to emerge from the Gulf crisis so far with any credit is the BBC and I should like to acknowledge the excellence of their World Service and in particular the *Gulf Link* programme.' Another, writing in Baghdad on the eve of her departure said:

'It was at times our only lifeline to the real world. In hiding, surrounded by Iraqi soldiers, Chris Loosemore's voice epitomised all that was imperishably dear to me. At my lowest point, shortly after capture, when I thought we would sooner or later all be killed, *Gulf Link* was my only comfort. Thanks again. PS. It will be good to listen to *The Archers* again.' And a man expressing 'our deepest appreciation' on behalf of himself and his wife added: 'We hope that you never have to broadcast a programme like *Gulf Link* again.'

Audiences in the United States also increased. The Arab network of America carried programmes every day from the Arabic Service. American Public Radio saw a rise in the number of stations taking the World Service from 75 to about 100. An estimated two million people listened each week on public radio. It was available on ringmain at the United Nations and in the State Department. In New Zealand re-broadcasts of World Service on FM 24 hours a day were started.

The troops waiting to invade Iraq also

listened. The firm of Sony donated 100 short wave radios to the 7th Armoured Brigade, the 'Desert Rats' so they could tune to the BBC and keep in touch. Harold Briley, the Bush House Defence Correspondent at the time, visited the Gulf in November 1990 and found the servicemen very appreciative of the BBC, although they said they would like not to have to switch frequencies trying to find it.. 'Flying with RAF Tornado pilots over the desert, I've watched them listening to me on World Service, reporting on their activities,' he told the staff newspaper, *Ariel*. 'Royal Navy personnel on patrol in the Gulf also listen regularly.'

The Commander of the British forces, General Sir Peter de la Billière, told Harold Briley in an interview: 'Obviously at the present time we are totally reliant on the BBC Overseas Service. And I mean this most sincerely, it is a marvellous service, and I certainly have the news on twice a day. And that's where I get a lot of my information.'

Less predictably, perhaps, there was praise from the Americans as well. The Commander

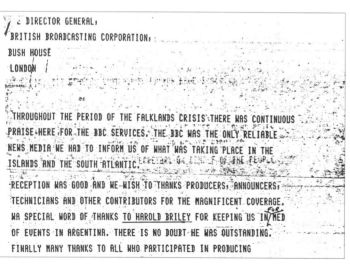

THE DIRECTOR GENERAL,
BRITISH BROADCASTING CORPORATION,
BUSH HOUSE
LONDON

THROUGHOUT THE PERIOD OF THE FALKLANDS CRISIS THERE WAS CONTINUOUS PRAISE HERE FOR THE BBC SERVICES. THE BBC WAS THE ONLY RELIABLE NEWS MEDIA WE HAD TO INFORM US OF WHAT WAS TAKING PLACE IN THE ISLANDS AND THE SOUTH ATLANTIC.
RECEPTION WAS GOOD AND WE WISH TO THANKS PRODUCERS, ANNOUNCERS, TECHNICIANS AND OTHER CONTRIBUTORS FOR THE MAGNIFICENT COVERAGE. WA SPECIAL WORD OF THANKS TO HAROLD BRILEY FOR KEEPING US INFORMED OF EVENTS IN ARGENTINA. THERE IS NO DOUBT HE WAS OUTSTANDING. FINALLY MANY THANKS TO ALL WHO PARTICIPATED IN PRODUCING

Praise indeed: H.T. Rowlands, financial secretary writing on behalf of the people of the Falkland Islands, thanks the BBC overseas service for their coverage of the conflict. Right, a letter from the Falkland Club at Port Stanley pays fulsome tribute.

150th ANNIVERSARY

FALKLAND CLUB,
Stanley,
Falkland Islands,
19th October, 1982.

To Harold Briley, Esq. (B.B.C. London),
Stanley, Falkland Islands.

This presentation is made to you by the Members of the Falkland Club in appreciation of your heartening reports from Buenos Aires during the Falklands conflict from 2nd April to 14th June, 1982. The fact that you operated in the heart of enemy territory at considerable risk to your safety, impressed us immensely. It was indeed a courageous effort which did a lot to boost the morale of the Falklanders during that very trying and dangerous period. We, Sir, will never forget you.

CHAIRMAN.

In July, 1982, Argentine vehicles litter the street outside the office of the Falkland Islands Company at Port Stanley.

of the US Sixth Fleet, Admiral J.D. Williams, said: 'It's good all-round objective news in most cases...At least a couple of times a day I listen to your BBC. It keeps me informed about everything really – about our budget crisis in Congress as well as the Gulf crisis, as well as all crises.' The World Service was regularly broadcast throughout the US aircraft carrier *Saratoga*. And a naval captain on board an amphibious landing ship delivered himself of this rather doubtful compliment: 'It's the BBC that some of us tend to prefer...Maybe it's hearing the British accent, it adds a little flavour, maybe a little bit of romance that reminds us of things we've seen in the movies.'

The British accent was to the fore in a

war just under ten years earlier – the war for the Falklands. The Argentine invasion of the islands took place two days after the Spanish service to Europe had been abolished as part of the economies demanded to pay for the audibility programme, and the Brazilian service in Portuguese had been cut.

The government asked the BBC to increase its Spanish service to Latin America but did not restore the cuts in the Brazilian service nor resurrect the Spanish service to Spain. In addition, the Ministry of Defence took over one of the BBC's frequencies to conduct psychological warfare by radio propaganda against members of the Argentine garrison.

But, according to an Argentine radio-producer posted temporarily to the

145

Falklands, hardly any of them had access to radio sets and he never met anybody who had heard the broadcasts.

The Argentine government jammed the Spanish transmissions and later those in English, but the jamming was not very successful and both services could still be heard; there was evidence of widespread listening. Radio stations in Argentina contacted the Latin American service in London for interviews until a decree was issued forbidding them to do so. Stations in neighbouring countries continued to use BBC material. The director of a station in Chile said it was far more objective than the material from Argentina which was 'sheer propaganda.'

As it was later to do in the Gulf crisis, the BBC reported Argentine statements and claims without comment. They were often untruthful and misleading, but this was not immediately apparent. And sometimes, particularly when it came to ship losses, they were accurate and ahead of the British. The lessons learned painfully during the Second World War –- be first with news of disasters and take defence correspondents into your confidence – had been completely forgotten by the military authorities in London.

The even-handed approach of the BBC had its vociferous critics at home. The World Service in particular was criticised for allegedly giving away details of the planned attack on Goose Green by 2 Parachute Battalion, an episode in which I was involved.

On the morning of 27 May, the capture of Goose Green was reported by the London *Daily Express*. This, as it turned out, was premature – Goose Green was not finally captured until the following day. The story was not confirmed by the Ministry of Defence spokesman who said, however, that he did not want to give the impression that nothing was happening.

A senior member of the Ministry of Defence gave Christopher Lee, defence

'Psst – What's the BBC saying, Sir?' The Argentine authorities were concerned enough during the Falklands conflict to start jamming. This brave cartoon appeared in La Prensa in April, 1982.

correspondent for BBC radio, details of the attack on Goose Green, which he thought was already in progress and therefore no secret. By the afternoon of 27 May this story was broadcast and the whole country knew about it, including the fact that there had already been a clash some five miles from Darwin – on the way to Goose Green.

In the Commons that afternoon Mrs Thatcher would only confirm that British forces had begun to move forward from their bridgehead, while all the military experts retained by the media knew exactly where the troops were headed, and said so publically.

The same afternoon the World Service reported some of these developments – rather cautiously – and a few days later was bitterly criticised in a despatch from a journalist in the Falklands for allegedly showing 'a reckless disregard for security' in mentioning troop positions. The allegation was investigated and rebutted at the time, by the Ministry of Defence as well as the BBC, but it emerged ten years later in a particularly virulent form in the memoirs of the task-force commander, Admiral Sandy Woodward. Of course, the troops in the Falklands could not know what was being reported in London and may well have felt exposed by the broadcast, although the report was actually broadcast *after* the clash with the Argentine patrol outside Darwin; hardly a breach of security for the Agentinians to be informed by the BBC after the event. The incident, though, is a reminder of the immediacy of radio, particularly noticeable in war.

After the Normandy landings in 1944, when strict military censorship was in force, a BBC correspondent was publically accused by General Omar Bradley of endangering American lives by reporting the advance on Falaise. The correspondent later received an apology.

On the other hand the World Service was also credited with bringing the war to an end. A Brazilian newspaper quoted an Argentine military chaplain as saying that the commander, General Mario Menéndez, defied orders to fight on after hearing news of the situation from the BBC, Uruguay and Chile. These two countries were relaying the BBC Latin American service, so presumably this is what General Menéndez, who spoke no English, was hearing.

By chance the BBC had for years been running a special programme called *Calling the Falklands*, a weekly compilation of record requests for the islanders. After the Argentine invasion, this became a regular transmission of news of interest to the islanders, a press review, extracts from Parliamentary debates and personal messages from friends and relatives, not only in Britain but from many other countries. A 15-minute programme became a 30-minute one, then a 45-minute one, including weekends. The programme continued like this for three months after the liberation, being cut eventually to two half hours a week. It was used by members of the government, the Archbishop of Canterbury,

the governor, Sir Rex Hunt (who was in Britain) and others to speak directly to the islanders, to keep their spirits up. A voice that was welcomed was that of Harold Briley, then the BBC Latin America correspondent.

Harold Briley was in Buenos Aires when Argentine forces invaded the islands, and he continued to report developments from there throughout the crisis. He had visited the Falklands and knew many of the people there. He began to broadcast a regular talk to them, two minutes a week in his friendly north-country accent. A few months after the end of the war he accompanied a Foreign Office minister, Cranley Onslow, on the first ministerial visit.

' We drove through Port Stanley, and there was a big banner across the street saying: "God bless you, Harold" he recalled later. Cranley Onslow asked: 'Is that Harold Wilson?' His puzzlement was soon dispelled. Harold Briley got down from the Land Rover. Men shook his hand, women kissed him, children asked for his autograph. He was given honorary membership of the Falklands Islands Committee. 'Your newsletters were a source of great comfort to us in our darkest days' said the invitation. He had a similar reception in other parts of the islands.

In an interview with him the governor, Sir Rex Hunt, paid him a personal tribute and illustrated the value of the link with Britain represented by *Calling the Falklands*. After describing the efforts of many of the islanders under Argentine occupation, Sir Rex went on: 'At the risk of embarrassing you, I'd like to say what a terrific job you did, and Peter King, from *Calling the Falklands* in London, to keep the spirits up of the people in the islands here. All of them have told me how helpful your recordings were from Buenos Aires. They've said how you managed to escape from being hung, drawn and quartered by the Argentines during the occupation they don't know...'

CHAPTER SIXTEEN

World Service Television

AT SEVEN O'CLOCK in the evening on 11 March 1991 the first World Service Television news bulletin went on the air with a version of *Lilliburlero*, the tune that has introduced World Service radio bulletins for many years. It led with pictures of rival pro- and anti-government demonstrations in Belgrade, a harbinger of far worse things to come. Other headlined stories covered one of the American Secretary of State's many visits to Israel to discuss Middle East peace talks, a meeting of OPEC ministers and the plight of Albanian refugees in Brindisi. Among other items was an interview with the Secretary-General of the Commonwealth, to mark Commonwealth Day. The bulletin had a pronounced international flavour.

On BBC1 the six o'clock news on the same evening led with a story about virgin births. Women who did not want sex with men were enabled to have a baby by artificial insemination at a clinic in Birmingham. There was comment from various parties ('reducing motherhood to animal husbandry' was one) and a statement by a government minister to the effect that the welfare of the child must be considered. The only headline common to both bulletins was the one about the American Secretary of State in Israel. Two television newsrooms were working to completely different agendas.

The Managing Director of World Service, John Tusa, described the opening as the most important event in World Service history since the launch of the Empire Service in 1932. The aim, he said, was to repeat on television the success already achieved on radio.

The day had been a long time in coming. As long ago as 1968 the then Director of External Broadcasting, Charles Curran (later to be Director-General), had mused about the possibility of using satellites to send radio and television abroad. In a paper which seems to have been circulated to only a handful of people he discussed the technical and financial problems. He said that for the BBC to launch its own satellites would cost about 40 million pounds. He concluded that direct television broadcasting from satellites was not viable in the current circumstances and that using satellites to send programmes to other broadcasters would probably be restricted to news, current affairs and actuality material.

Television technology progressed swiftly

and 16 years later, in February 1984, a successor to Charles Curran, Douglas Muggeridge, Managing Director of External Broadcasting (as it was still called), decided that the time had come to launch a television service. He went to the United States to make his ideas public, apparently receiving a rap over the knuckles for sounding off without informing his superiors. (This was at a time when the BBC, having announced that it was going to undertake direct broadcasting by satellite, was finding that it would be too expensive.)

He told the Los Angeles World Affairs Council that a start ought to be made with a service for cable operators and re-broadcasting by foreign stations; in the long run the objective would be a direct service for the world, like the one on radio. 'The competition is already building up,' he said. 'We need to act quickly.'

Eighteen months later the Director-General commissioned a working party to study the issue; the working party concluded there was a need for an urgent examination of the subject in detail. By now it was January 1986 and it took another five months to set up a steering group which in turn commissioned a planning team. Now things were finally moving, and by August 1986 the team came up with a recommendation for a daily half hour news programme to be sent by satellite to foreign broadcasters and cable operators who would constitute, according to the planning team's report, a substantial market although the income would not be enough to cover the costs in the early years.

The BBC applied to the Foreign Office for the money for a service costing £7.8 million a year, plus £1.4 million for the initial capital cost; this would be for a number of editions each day on various satellites.

Bush House sent its formidable lobbying machine into action and no fewer than 230 MPs signed an Early Day Motion calling on the government to find the money. BBC lore

is that it was Mrs Thatcher who vetoed the use of government money. She was said to dislike BBC television intensely, so was hardly likely to back a second television service, in spite of her admiration for the World Service.

But the BBC case was fatally weakened in the government's eyes anyway by the fact that Independent Television News had already started an international news service which was going out by satellite on Superchannel – a service which has since been brought to an end.

Revised proposals were put to the Foreign Office; just one programme a day, only £3.4 million. However, in March 1988, in a statement in Parliament, a junior Foreign Office Minister (Tim Eggar) announced that nothing would be forthcoming. 'We note that a British commercial world television news service has been started without public funds' (he said) 'and have concluded that the provision of public funds to the BBC for this purpose would not be justified.'

A letter of August, 1991, from the Prime Minister congratulates the BBC world service on the effectiveness of their broadcasts in the Russian service.

Enter the graphic designer. Television demands that the visual elements complement the spoken word.

Apparently the BBC had no advance warning of this statement which cannot, however, have come as a complete surprise. And Mr Eggar did add that the government would not stop the BBC from taking the initiative.

This it proceeded to do. Up to now it had been thinking in terms of public service broadcasting paid for by the government at least to start the process; later it would start earning money. But the announcement in Parliament alerted a number of entrepreneurs who expressed interest in the service. Finally the BBC selected a merchant bank, J Henry Schroder, to prepare a business plan. World Service TV was going commercial.

Alan Macdonald from the newsroom in Bush House, had been one of the original planning team (he later became Head of Business Development). When the team disbanded he stayed at Television Centre to continue the work of putting the service on the air. 'It was like running an embassy in a largely hostile environment,' he said later. 'I had one or two friends who supported the notion, but the vast majority were sceptical.' One problem was that many people in

television felt that if there were to be a service at all they should be running it, not Bush House.

The business plan produced by Schroders said in effect that the service could be launched commercially providing certain conditions were met; the most important of these was acquisition of global rights to pictures from Visnews and the National Broadcasting Company of America (NBC). A long period of negotiations followed. Visnews, which is partly owned by the BBC, was concerned that if its pictures were sent around the world by satellite, its existing subscribers would simply lift them and become former subscribers. To avoid this the BBC made it clear that such 'stripping' would not be allowed.

Once agreement had been reached the Board of Governors approved the project in June, 1990. It then became necessary to appoint a Chief Executive who would have the qualities of 'an educated hustler.' After various formalities Chris Irwin, then at Bush House but with previous experience in television was selected. Because of the delays of the previous five years it was not possible to start the service until early in 1991. John Tusa commented: 'It is now recognised that for Britain not to have been in the international TV news business during the Gulf crisis was a major strategic error. We are now putting that right as fast as we can.'

The fact that the American Cable News Network (CNN) received so much exposure during the Gulf crisis through its presence in Baghdad was particularly galling; it is seen as a network catering primarily for the American audience, not a truly international one. The Gulf War seems to have been a factor in the decision finally to launch the service, another the need to be seen to be doing something in Europe in 1992. There may also be a third factor: a way of preserving the BBC in the run-up to the renewal of its charter in 1996 would be to have a good international television news service which largely depended on the resources of the BBC at home. If you damage or destroy the BBC at home, you damage or destroy it abroad. This, of course, has always been true of radio, but nowadays discussion of the future of the BBC is mainly conducted in terms of its television service.

Whatever the reasons, World Service television went ahead. BBC Enterprises, which provided the working capital, also bequeathed its services to Europe, both on satellite (BBC TV Europe) and by direct transmission to cable companies in nearby countries which provided it with immediate income. Although the first news bulletin went out on 11 March the service proper did not start until a month later – 15 April – with news, business reports, global weather, a selection of programmes from BBC1 and BBC2 and English lessons from BBC English (formerly called *English by Radio and Television*).

The BBC has been in the business of teaching English for nearly 50 years, since July 1943. At that time, in the middle of the war, news was still the main consideration and there was little time for lessons – a few periods of five minutes early in the morning in some foreign languages to help people already studying English. They proved popular; at the end of the war German troops in Norway heard an announcement that they were to lay down their arms which was flashed into an English lesson they were listening to on the German Service.

With the coming of peace what had begun as an experiment was put on an organised basis. A special department was set up to produce English lessons for broadcasting. It had advice from experts in teaching English as a foreign language. As a complement to the broadcasts it produced records with accompanying booklets. In 1962 it moved into television as well.

BBC English now earns more than any other department in the World Service; it plans to increase its revenue from £2 million in 1990 to £5 million by 1995. It continues its direct broadcasting by radio and has also produced a large number of audio-cassettes for re-broadcasting all over the world. One course teaches English by explaining the words of pop songs; it has been broadcast in over 30 countries. Another gives help with pronunciations.

English-speaking bears are rare, but Muzzy is quite fluent and helps teach children all over the world.

Tough trail in search of tropical news

by LIZ BLUNT

THURSDAY: A producer phones me in Abidjan and suggests the West Africa Correspondent might like to contribute a four minute feature to the next BBC World News television pilot the following week.

I suggest the start of a big constitutional review in Nigeria, discussing how to return to civilian rule. After all, I had just completed two weeks with television training on the special TV News course at Elstree at the end of my last leave from Bush House, and it all looked so easy.

Managed to get through to Nigeria to a good contact, press secretary to the Chief of Staff, supreme headquarters — Nigeria's military prime minister.

He is highly delighted. Says what a good idea. Of course I don't need a special permit. And the crew? No problem.

FRIDAY: The producer says go and do it. Cancel my next week's appointments, water the plants and get a ticket to get me to Lagos by 8.30 Sunday evening.

SUNDAY, 8.30pm: Still at Abidjan Airport. Air Afrique has gone past without stopping (due to a tropical downpour) and will have to come back and pick us up later. Arrive at Lagos Airport at 3am, six and a half hours late.

Remember all the stories of the robber-infested road from airport to town. Problem largely solved by immigration, who take one and a half hours to clear me — by which time all armed robbers are probably sleeping the sleep of the unjust.

MONDAY: Ring my contact who says to come right over. He's a very charming,

elegant northern Nigerian in spotless white robes.

We take tea, discuss the state of Nigeria, the BBC etc.

But what about the crew? Ah, he says, the crew. Well, unfortunately they are being a little greedy. They want £10,000 per day paid in sterling. But no problem, there are others.

I tell them my limit. My contact looks pained.

I set out for the airport to get my four cassettes sent out from London. At the cargo shed I am instantly mobbed by about 15 men waving identity cards and claiming to be clearing agents.

Make firmly for the British Caledonian office pursued by the mob, who attempt to force their way in after me. B-Cal chase them out, barricade the door and

confirm the package has arrived. Unfortunately it is too late to start clearing it that day . . .

Now late afternoon. I still have no crew and no tapes, and the tropical downpour has followed me to Lagos. I get directed to a new film company who offer a crew with high-band equipment.

TUESDAY 0630: Still raining.

Go to see my friend and explain I want pictures of the military state house, Dodon Barracks and the old colonial state house on Marina. Is he sure I don't need some kind of mission? He looks reproachful. Nigeria, he says, is a free country.

Go and talk to the Ministry of Information, who are absolutely horrified. Of course I need a permit. Why didn't I let them know last month? I'm referred to the ultimate authority, who rules that everyone is right. I don't officially need a permit, but no policeman on duty is likely to know this. Finally emerge with a permit handwritten on presidential notepaper.

WEDNESDAY: Filming day. The sun is shining and it's dry — important since large parts of Lagos flood, and vehicles disappear into craters of water when it rains.

Arrive at the film company.

The Number Two, a man called Innocent, tells me the crew is there (marvellously punctual). They are just over the road, getting their gear together.

But just one thing. Did I want high-band? Oh, because they hadn't remembered to charge their high-band batteries. I get very angry, but he promises alternatives. I subsequently learn that this crew did not exist at all.

The alternative turns out to be a crew with all its high-band batteries out on another job. But it does exist. So it is suggested. we shoot the exteriors low-band in the morning, and convert them in the afternoon while we shoot the interviews on mains power. We agree a price to include a small boy to carry the gear.

By 1100 we finally get started. Dodon Barracks turns out to be easy. But at the old state house disaster strikes. Despite the permit we are confined to the guardhouse for one-and-a-half hours, and then told no pictures.

At the National Assembly, police and security guards announce filming is forbidden. We produce the permit, but they need a photocopy . . . I rapidly rewrite my piece to camera so it can be said somewhere else.

By now it's very late and we

are clearly not going to get to the constitutional lawyer, Rotimi Williams, by three. The cameraman wants to go get shots of street scenes, but I overrule him on the grounds that Chief Williams didn't get to be the best-paid lawyer in Nigeria by sloppy timekeeping.

Raise the question of lunch, but the crew favours pressing on. The small boy looks wistful.

The interview goes well, enlivened by the realisation that if we simply clip the mike to his robes we are going to have an ugly black wire stretching across his ample frontage. I modestly turn my back while the crew wrestles with the problem of getting the mike up inside his flowing garment.

Do another interview but it's 6 o'clock and getting dark. We have no street scenes, nor have I done by P to Cs. I have Sandy McCourt's training lectures ringing in my ears. He's going to be very disappointed with this pupil.

Find a deserted street and start doing them. The evening rush hour starts, with commuters interrupting every time I get to the third sentence.

By 6.30 the light has gone. The cameraman expresses admiration for the BBC in general, me in particular and asks my room number and whether I have a husband. I deflect the conversation . . .

The small boy says he is tired and hungry and if this is what television news is like, he doesn't think much of it.

I secretly agree.

Elizabeth Blunt

West Africa correspondent

Now working for the World Television Service, Elizabeth Blunt and her recording crew run into a little difficulty.

Television is an expensive medium, particularly in colour, so here BBC English has looked for partners to defray the cost and ensure the operation remains self-financing. A programme called *Follow Me*, for example, was produced in collaboration with West German television and the Council of Europe. Described in *The Economist* as 'the most widely followed teaching course in history', *Follow Me* is a two -year course for beginners which has been seen in more than 70 countries, either on television or in the classroom. A new version is being produced.

Other productions for television include dramas and cartoons. *Muzzy in Gondoland*, which first saw the light in 1988, is about a friendly monster who comes from outer space.

It features various other characters, good and bad, to provide an adventure story which also gives children a command of basic English vocabulary and structures. It has been shown in many European countries, and in Russia. Later came a follow-up course – *Muzzy Comes Back*.

Although learning English from television can be entertaining, World Service TV received some unwelcome publicity soon after it opened. There were complaints from British viewers watching cable television in France. The programmes they were used to watching, such as *Neighbours*, Wimbledon and local news, had been replaced. A Briton working in Paris expostulated: 'It is absolutely appalling....we call it the rage channel because it makes us all so angry.' The head of BBC Enterprises, James Arnold-Baker, was quoted as saying :'Although the expatriates are a vociferous bunch who have been drowning out the praise we have won from many other viewers, I am afraid we are not going to be able to change. I accept that they may have a point. However, relaying everything from BBC1 and BBC2 is not what we are about.'

Broadcasting to Europe was a start, but it

was not enough by itself. In October, World Service television took a long step forward with a news and information channel for Asia. This was the result of an agreement with a Hong-Kong based company, HutchVision, who run a satellite television service, Star TV (Satellite Television Asian Region).

The service is beamed to 38 countries, and the potential audience amounts to half the world's population. However, as a spokesman for Star TV put it: 'We are talking about the top 5% of Asians, who travel frequently and have in common their money, their Mercedes and the English language.'

They can receive it with their own dish aerials or through cable or re-broadcasts, although the nature of many governments in the region makes the latter problematic. In India, for example, cable and satellite are technically illegal. This did not stop entrepreneurs erecting dish aerials to receive CNN and selling the service to subscribers. When the BBC service began it produced hundreds of enquiries.

Star TV also transmits other channels, such as sport (Prime Network International from the USA) and music (MTV). It relies entirely on advertising for its income, and the BBC programmes incorporate breaks for commercials which are added in Hong Kong.

BBC world service news presenters can smile, even in Shepherds Bush. Back row (left to right), Brian Empringham, Riz Khan, Jack Thompson. Front row (left to right), Juliet Alexander, Lynette Lithgow, Christabel King, Alison Rooper, Pamela Armstrong, Verity Spencer, Tanya Sillem.

The BBC has the right of veto over any commercial it considers might bring its image or reputation into disrepute. Its costs are covered and it shares any surplus, which is for ploughing back into programmes. By being one stage removed from the actual business of selling advertising it is free of its pressures. Even so the arrangement means that the BBC has, almost unnoticed, gone commercial. With this example, there will be renewed calls for its domestic service to take advertising to replace or supplement the licence fee.

The co-operation with Star TV provides a 24-hour news and news-related service for Asia, which includes such domestic BBC programmes as *Panorama* and *40 minutes*. 'We're not just a one-parent family,' as Chris Irwin puts it. He has committed himself to seeking a presence in every continent by 1993. The idea is to identify possible partners in different parts of the globe and negotiate a deal which enables the BBC to retain editorial control and match editorial skills to commercial strength. He sees CNN as complementary to the World Service rather than as competition. In a speech to the Singapore Press Club in September 1991 he said: 'CNN has built up a justified reputation for being there as things happen... Our strength is different. The BBC is renowned for the depth of its journalism and for its commitment to impartiality, its respect for the intelligence of its audience.' There is another argument: 'Two reasons to buy a satellite dish are better than one; the existence of both the BBC and CNN will encourage people to buy the necessary receiving equipment. Our co-existence is mutually beneficial.'

After the service began, people started telephoning from various parts of the world to find out more.

A man in Darwin, Australia, wanted to know if he could get it. Gail Styles of the newsroom recalls a rather secretive long-distance caller who said he had been enjoying the programmes. It turned out that

The news gallery at the BBC World Service Television centre, Wood Lane, where controllers monitor and assemble programmes for transmission around the world.

An operator at the control desk of the World Service Television.

he came from near Moscow. In fact, several stations in what was the Soviet Union broadcast the service, as well as those in other countries of East and Central Europe; some of them dub it in their own languages.

The newsroom is a blend of 'two cultures', the knowledge of, and sensitivity to, foreign audiences (or 'intellectual arrogance' as one person put it – perhaps only half humorously) of Bush House and the technical skills of *Television News*. The editor, Johan Ramsland, is from Bush House, the managing editor, John Exelby, from television, and the rest of the staff are also drawn from the two traditions. The presenters are suitably multi-racial. The news studio is in Television Centre. The newsroom uses the BBC's own correspondents as well as Visnews and NBC

material and has been training radio correspondents in the mysteries of television – the buzz-word now is 'bi-media'.

World Service Television is still in its early stages. It has ground to make up, not only on CNN but on French and Italian channels. Apart from news, it does not make its own programmes yet but depends on BBC1 and BBC2, which look primarily to the domestic audience. Nevertheless, Chris Irwin is confident: 'We have the BBC name, which is the strongest brand label in world broadcasting. We have the English language teaching programmes of the specialist World Service department, *BBC English*, which are a major attraction. And we have *World Service Television News*, which is the jewel in the crown.'

CHAPTER SEVENTEEN

Into the Nineties

IN 1984 the Foreign Secretary appointed a
team to look into the efficiency of the
External Services. It included representatives
of the Foreign and Commonwealth Office,
the External Services themselves and the firm
of consultants Deloitte, Haskins and Sells; it
was headed by a man from the Treasury,
Alan Perry. The Perry report said that Bush
House placed great importance on editorial
and engineering skills but ought to concentrate more on management skills. In particular
it ought to tell the FCO more about where
the money went.

A particularly critical paragraph said: 'It is
disturbing that currently the FCO is not in a
position to judge, except in the broadest terms
by comparison with the total costs of other
programmes, whether the costs quoted by the
BBC for any extra transmission are realistic
or not. There was, for example, considerable
concern within the FCO about the additional
costs which the BBC calculated they would
incur in increasing transmissions to Latin
America and the Falklands in 1982, but this
was not pursued in detail with the BBC,
since the FCO had no firm basis on which to
query them.'

The report published a new statement of

objectives which the World Service agreed
with the FCO. It should, it said, enhance
Britain's standing abroad and form among
listeners a better understanding of the UK.
To do this it must provide a credible, unbiased,
reliable, accurate, balanced and independent
news service; give a balanced view of
national and international developments;
represent British life accurately and effectively;
and increase the understanding and speaking
of English. It made a number of recommendations – for example, the FCO should
monitor how the BBC meets its objectives,
although without affecting its editorial
independence; middle and senior management
should have more training in managing
resources, the grant-in-aid should be determined at the same time as the licence fee for the
rest of the Corporation and for the same
period, the External Services should provide
more financial and management information
to the FCO.

John Tusa, who became Managing
Director in 1986, had the task of putting into
effect the ensuing managerial revolution. 'It
was quite clear at the time,' he said, 'that the
general impression in the Foreign Office was
that we were soft on money and that because

we were soft, cases for further funding didn't stand much of a chance.'

The report had called for the introduction of a new priority-based budgetary system without saying what form it should take; the BBC asked Deloitte, Haskins and Sells to devise one. They came back with a detailed plan. Although it was only a short time before the new budgetary negotiations were due to begin with the Foreign Office, it was decided to put the new system into effect right away. 'I think the most important decision I have taken was to decide we couldn't bring it in 15 months later,' John Tusa says. 'Now that we had it on the table we had to do it. There was a lot of unease, a lot of uncertainty and head-shaking, but I and enough of my colleagues agreed we had to go ahead.'

The essence of the system is 'setting objectives for the World Service and for each department, costing the department's activities and relating them to the objectives, identifying and costing possible changes to existing activities and prioritising those changes.' It has made savings possible, identified inefficiencies and given the World

Service the ability to re-allocate money from its own resources, so 'if we want to do something new we don't have to go running to the Foreign Office' in John Tusa's words. The decision to broadcast in Ukrainian is an example.

One result of the Perry report is that the grant-in-aid is settled over a three-year period, like the licence fee, with allowances for inflation. For the triennium from 1991 to 1994 Bush House mounted a considerable exercise, setting out its principles and aims, not just for the three years but beyond – a touch of what President Bush described as 'the vision thing.' Preparing it took nearly a year, and there were another five months of negotiation with the Foreign Office. The agreed proposals were then put to the Treasury, which turned down some of them. In spite of that the World Service came out with an increase of six per cent in real terms to improve programmes – the first time government money had been given for that purpose and an indirect reward perhaps for greater financial acountability.

The basis of the BBC's argument was that 'Britain has in the World Service the world's

Ex-Manchester United star, Bobby Charlton, being honoured on the French for Africa *programme.*

A 1989 broadcast to Russia included Sam Yossman's interview with ex-Beatle Paul McCartney.

John Tusa at a BBC World Service breakfast with Vaclav Havel, President of Czechoslovakia, in March, 1990.

most listened-to and most trusted international broadcasting organisation. We will build on the success already achieved...'
It also stressed the need to give value for money and even suggested at one point that its credibility might be 'quantifiable' as a 'performance indicator.' The outcome of the negotiations was described as 'a tremendous vote of confidence in the role of World Service radio' by John Tusa. Broadcasting in Sinhala for Sri Lanka was restored after fifteen years. The hours of the Russian, Chinese and Vietnamese services were increased, but the Japanese and Malay services were abolished. Both had tiny audiences – about 20,000 in the case of Malay – and no lobby was mounted in their defence.

The five years up to 1991 showed, as well as a change in the culture of management, considerable changes in programming, in English as well as foreign languages. One was a change of name. The title World Service,

originally confined to the service in English, was extended to services in foreign languages in 1988, supplanting the term External Services. It was a change that had been mooted (and resisted) for some time. People outside the BBC called it the World Service anyway, whatever language it was in.

One problem with the World Service in English was that it was viewed nostalgically by many listeners as a haven of good, old-fashioned values; it was in danger of appearing quaint, almost eccentric, in a world where radio was changing rapidly. The manager of a radio station in Barbados explained in 1986 why his station had stopped re-broadcasting it; listeners in the Caribbean, he said, preferred the slicker, more colloquial style of Voice of America to what was seen as the stuffy approach of the BBC. Research confirmed that there was a problem. Asked to describe the World Service as a person, people in various

158

countries gave replies such as: 'conservative, not too exciting, does not like changes'; 'the aunt who is at times very serious, at times very funny, a bit whimsical.' An internal report in 1987 concluded: 'World Service is informative and educative but too often dull, dutiful and mechanical. There is much respect for news and current affairs programmes, there is also criticism of style and presentation. We do not sound contemporary, we do not sound attractive.'

A process called World Service Renewal was gradually implemented over a period of two years. 'Programmes were reshaped as the opportunity arose, voices were replaced as the opportunity occurred.

Much had already been changed quietly, without fanfare, when it was decided to unveil World Service Renewal to the press in October 1988.' (John Tusa, *Conversations with the World*, BBC Books, 1990). The ensuing publicity produced a number of indignant letters. 'I fervently wish Mrs Thatcher could step in and take control,' said one. 'I deplore the arrogance that leads you to suppose that you know better what is good for people....' said another. John Tusa concluded: 'What was revealing was that the overwhelming majority wrote on the basis of

what they had been told would happen rather than on the basis of experience... Next time we will simply introduce the changes and leave the audience to find out for themselves. If they don't notice, then we must have got it right.'

A system of evaluation was set up for language services. Three days output of a service is recorded, then translated back into English. A dozen people from various departments, including the service being evaluated and led by John Tusa, then spend the best part of a day going through the output. They compare the translation with the original English and look at editorial standards. They make recommendations which are followed up by service heads and controllers. Up to the winter of 1991, thirty services had been evaluated and, John Tusa says, 'there were very few cases where we did not call for a significant improvement in journalism – and got it.'

Some people got hurt in the process of change. There were redundancies as well as resignations on the part of people who were out of sympathy with the new thinking. Not everybody is happy with the fact that coverage of news and current affairs has increased so that they now account for just

A member of the Urdu service talks to Bangladeshi refugees at this makeshift camp.

Another kind of refugee, Salman Rushdie, being inter-viewed on the BBC World Service, before the fatwa.

over half the total output. However, it is planned to spend more on other types of programme.

In 1988 the BBC resumed its daily service to the Caribbean. This had been abolished in 1974 as part of the cuts imposed by the government and several previous attempts had been made to restore it. *Caribbean Report* is a live, 15 minute programme which goes out every day from Monday to Friday.

It is re-broadcast by some 28 stations in the Caribbean as well as being available in the United States through American Public Radio. There is also a weekly taped programme, *Caribbean Magazine*, featuring news about the Caribbean community in Britain.

In 1991 the English service to Europe returned after a long absence. It had started just before the war, been abolished in one of the many postwar cuts and now returned with 1992 in mind, although its brief extended beyond the EEC into Eastern Europe and Scandinavia.

The World Service has now acquired the equivalent of a written constitution or

Staff members of the Tamil language programme grace the steps at the entrance to Bush House.

Waiting for the driver. The BBC bus, a London double-decker, ready to travel overseas to promote the World Service.

perhaps, to change the metaphor, a creed to live by. Its plan for 1991-92 began with a 'vision', a mission statement and a list of objectives, followed by a list of individual services with their budgets and key targets. The vision is described as follows: 'Free and untainted information is a basic human right. Not everyone has it; almost everyone wants it. It cannot by itself create a just world, but a just world order can never exist without it. The BBC World Service aims to be trusted by its audience, independent of political partisanship and commercial pressures. It reflects the world to the world, promotes a common understanding and shared experience between people of different nationalities and culture.'

The mission statement describes how the World Service aims to set about being 'always credible, generally available and widely accessible' by broadcasting news, information, education and entertainment 'in many languages but one tone of voice';

reflecting its own society; using the best technical means available; monitoring foreign broadcasters; using public money efficiently; and finally looking after its staff and developing their talents. In case this is not considered enough, there is amplification in the form of a list of objectives, seven in all, covering much the same ground but in greater detail. This is perilously close to the sonorous declarations issued after international summit meetings – and is part of the same trend – but it has the merit of defining how the World Service sees its role and the standards it aspires to.

The future of the World Service – and of all international broadcasting– is governed partly by technical developments. The use of satellites for rebroadcasting has already been mentioned; it seems destined to become increasingly significant. The television link to Asia has enabled radio programmes to be beamed there as well. From November 1991 the satellite has carried BBC transmissions in

18 languages which can be rebroadcast on FM or cable or received direct by satellite dish in homes and public buildings such as hotels. The airline Cathay Pacific has fitted its aircraft with special aerials which can pick up the World Service wherever it happens to be. 'Rebroadcasting has been the kind of success nobody had dared to imagine,' according to Deputy Managing Director David Witherow, chairman of the rebroadcasting committee.

In the 21st century there could be greater use of satellites for radio through direct broadcasting. The controller of Overseas Services, Peter Udell, argued in 1990: 'Listeners all over the world could be tuning in to international broadcasters and getting as good reception as they get on their own local FM stations – if, that is, governments are prepared to pay the enormous costs of high powered direct broadcasting satellites, and if radio manufacturers are prepared to invest in new radio sets to receive the signals from satellites.'

The possibilities seem endless, but there is obviously a danger that with a proliferation of television and radio channels all over the world, particularly the developed world, there will simply be too much and standards will slip. More may mean worse. Another danger is of what is loosely described as cultural imperialism. American television already fills the screens of many countries, sometimes dubbed bizarrely into the local language. I have an abiding memory from some years ago of watching two American cowboys on television shouting at each other in Arabic. CNN is available by subscription in a number of countries. British television and radio programmes are also sold all over the world and, with the coming of World Service Television, will increasingly fill the screens of the better off everywhere.

The World Service denies that is in the business of cultural imperialism and, as international broadcasters go, it is probably

freer of it than most. An article on Bush House in the magazine *New Internationalist* in 1976 argued: 'A World Service programme is probably about as disinterested as a railway built by British colonial administrators for a population who would be bound to benefit and whose only mark of displeasure would be not to use it.' But it does not always look like that from the other end – from a Third World country, for example, which has to rely on a British interpretation of international events because it cannot afford its own analysts to do the job from its own perspective.

During the seventies there was a great deal of talk about a New World Information Order. Third World countries felt at a disadvantage because the international media, including the main news agencies, were largely in the hands of Western countries and reported with a Western bias. All that came out of Africa, for example, was news of coups, famines and natural disasters, entrenching the already existing belief in the West that nothing else happened there. The talk has now died down, partly because the agencies improved their performance but mainly because Western countries showed that the remedies proposed were worse than the disease in that they would have circumscribed press freedom. And as George Orwell put it immediately after the last war, 'Although other aspects of the question are usually in the foreground, the controversy over freedom of speech and of the press is at bottom a controversy over the desirability, or otherwise, of telling lies. What is really at issue is the right to report contemporary events truthfully, or as truthfully as is consistent with the ignorance, bias and self-deception from which every observer necessarily suffers.' (*The Prevention of Literature 1945-6* Penguin Books 1957)

The emphasis by the BBC on 'free and untainted information' is in the same vein. But, as the *New Internationalist* article quoted above put it: ' ....the BBC's "soft" democratic

Terry Waite was one of the several hostages whose captivity was made a little more bearable by the BBC World Service. Here, back in England after his ordeal, he talks to Barbara Myers about his experience.

image of Britain – indeed the very fact of putting across everything – warts-and all – is in itself ideological and reflective of British values; even propaganda, dare one say it, albeit subtle. And some people might find a certain irony in proclaiming the virtues of free information from Britain, which is hardly in the top league in that respect. The British have always favoured secrecy and decisions taken behind the scenes. In the United States information is seen as something publicly available unless there is good reason to withhold it. In Britain it is regarded as something to be withheld unless there is good reason to release it; usually because it is good public relations.

The *Newspaper Society*, which links owners of provincial newspapers, published a booklet in June 1991 which spoke of a

'paranoid requirement for secrecy' on the part of the government and said: 'In recent years...strenuous – almost ludicrous – efforts have been made to anticipate publication with gagging injunctions and to represent the press as distinct from, and even anti-pathetic to, the public interest. A formidable array of obstacles exists to prevent any embarrassment to the government of the day...'

The Spycatcher case was a notorious example of information freely available to the rest of the world being denied to people in Britain. A less well-known example is that of a young reporter on a trade magazine who tried to check his facts before publishing a story. He was heavily fined for refusing to disclose the source of his information and forbidden to publish it. In the words of the

Newspaper Society: 'To this day the identity of his adversary cannot be made known.'

As far as the BBC is concerned one of the obstacles is the prohibition on broadcasting directly the words of people assumed to be connected with Irish terrorism, including members of a political party, Sinn Fein, which is legal in Northern Ireland and receives a respectable share of the vote (13.4% in 1983, 11,4% in 1987).

Their words, however, can be reported or spoken by presenters, a situation which would have appealed to W.S. Gilbert or, for that matter Lewis Carroll. This ban, of course, has not resulted in fewer acts of terrorism; it means that the words of its supporters cannot be challenged on the air. It does not apply to people of other nationalities who justify terrorism, even when conducted against Britons.

Government action of this sort (and the Real Lives affair in 1985) weakens the credibility of the World Service by opening it to a 'how can you criticise our lack of freedom when you're not free yourself ?' type of response. But, of course, all things are relative. The diminution of press freedom in Britain is serious and needs to be reversed, but it does not compare – yet – with the lack of freedom in so many countries where listening to the BBC is widespread.

Since the ending of communism in Eastern Europe the idea of multi-party democracy has become fashionable, not only there but in other parts of the world as well.

But it is not unduly cynical to argue that, for many people, multi-party democracy is synonymous with Western affluence and, if they do not achieve the latter in a reasonable time, they will desert the former. Nationalism, smothered under communism, has re-appeared with ghastly consequences, for example, in Yugoslavia. The world is still a dangerous and unpredictable place.

In BBC terms that means not abolishing services to countries which now seem stable and well-disposed to Britain. The traditional argument still applies: international broadcasting cannot be turned on and off like a tap, it is essentially a long-term operation.

American hostage Tom Sutherland, after five years' captivity in Beirut, declared 'The BBC kept our minds alive'.

Transmissions to Eastern Europe need to remain, notwithstanding the changes. President Vaclav Havel of Czechoslovakia, for example, said during a visit to London in 1990 that it was very important that BBC broadcasts should continue as part of his country's change to democracy.

In the countries which undertake it, international broadcasting is paid for by the government. Although the World Service is generating a certain amount of income from such activities as teaching English, it can never be entirely self-supporting. Television may take advertising in Asia, but radio talks mainly to poorer people who are not of much interest to advertisers. In any case there would be dangers. If the BBC had been running advertisements in its Arabic service during the Gulf War, for example, commercial pressures might have been added to government complaints about its alleged bias in favour of Saddam Hussein.

Running the World Service for a year costs roughly the same as running the National Health Service for about two and a half days. Looked at another way, it is about one-sixtieth of the amount spent on buying defence equipment; you could get the best part of a frigate or seven or eight Tornado aircraft for the same money. Is it worth it? There is no obvious return for the outlay. No, says John Tusa, 'but there is a huge cultural invisible return; just because it can't be counted it doesn't mean the benefit

doesn't exist... It is inconceivable for a major country not to have this way of communicating with the world – it is far more central to international affairs now than anyone would once have thought possible – and our performance against our competitors shows we are far and away the best at doing it.'

Most would agree, including Mr Gorbachev and those Westerners held hostage for so many years and in such appalling conditions in Lebanon. Terry Waite said the World Service 'helped keep us alive both spiritually through the work of the religious departments and mentally through the variety of cultural and news programmes.' And the Scots-born American Thomas Sutherland, released with him, praised the Voice of America but added: 'I'm afraid I have to admit that the BBC has everybody beaten hands down.....I would guess that if one took a bunch of money...and said to a director: 'Put together the best kind of international radio you could devise', I think you would come up with something like the BBC .'

These comments are testimonies to the fact that, despite political pressures at home and abroad, and despite the 'ignorance, bias and self-delusion' to which all observers are naturally subject, the BBC is not falling too far short of the ideal purpose of international broadcasting: to provide a skyful of truth, a skyful of freedom.

The Story of Bush House

Mary Welch

From the offices of the architect, Harvey Corbett,
a working drawing of the Aldwych entrance to Bush
House published in *The Architectural Review*.

SAY 'BUSH' to any member of BBC staff and
it immediately conjures images of an imposing, if
not particularly elegant building at the southern
end of Kingsway in central London, fronted by
an enormous portico over which two male statues
reach towards each other, symbolising, we are told,
Anglo-American friendship. It is this building
which is home to the BBC World Service.

Although the grandeur of the exterior does not
extend very far inside, the entrance is impressive:
marble walls, wide staircases with marble treads
and some of the original bronze fittings remaining.

THE ARCHITECTURAL REVIEW.

THE ALDWYCH FRONT.

THE STRAND FRONT.

THE WEST FLANK OF BUSH HOUSE.
The Aldwych entrance is on the left, and that to the Strand on the right.

Bush House, photographed upon its completion in 1922, although the monument above the Aldwych portico is not yet in place. The later extensions, built to either side, mean that these views no longer exist.

Previously occupied by YMCA huts, this 1920 photograph shows that work on the foundations has started. Traffic-free Aldwych is in the foregound; beyond is St Clement Danes church in the Strand.

Once beyond this magnificence the offices are cramped and ventilation less than perfect. Bush House was never designed as the headquarters of a broadcasting organisation: the layout of the building is confusing and there are those who believe that no one can learn to confidently navigate around the four blocks in less than two years. It is, in spite of all these drawbacks, an enormously friendly building: office doors are usually wide open, there are casual encounters in the wide corridors and the BBC club and canteen are well established institutions. As a place to work it seems to inspire affection and irritation in roughly equal parts – with affection just gaining the edge.

The original site lay at the end of the tree-lined Kingsway Development to the Strand. It had been earmarked for development for a decade, but the difficulties involved in acquiring the surrounding property and building an underground 'tramway' made progress very slow. The Globe of 4 June 1903 fretted:

'Whoever suggested the hurried completion of these few yards of road and pavement at the corner near St. Clement Danes was a good salesman. It seems so much and is, in effect, so little; even Wych St is not yet out of the hands of the housebreaker.'

The Architechtural Review published several sets of plans and designs from 1900 as a group of American businessmen wanted to develop the site for offices, while Lord Grey proposed that the site be devoted to London offices for the Dominions. In the meantime the First World War broke out; the weeds continued to flourish and the site was used for YMCA huts instead.

It was not until October 1919 that the papers broke the glad news: the Aldwych site was to be let by the London County Council at a rent of £55,000 per annum to Irving T. (Ter) Bush, an American businessman. He was not, it seems, particularly well known in Lonon, and even today remains a shadowy figure. The bare facts of his life are given in Who's Who in America. Born Ridgeway, Michigan in 1869, the son of Rufus T. and Sarah M. Bush. He went into the family firm, Bush and Denslow Manufacturing, when he was nineteen, married three times, and died in October 1948.

He 'early became interested in relieving the congestion of business and traffic in New York'. A journalist who developed the bones of the story in 1937 described Bush's foundation of the Bush Terminal in New York, and how he saw the need for a similiar service in London – the foundation and development of a business centre 'wherein manufacturers took space in the form

169

This photograph was taken when the site was actually vacant, but a photograph of a model of the building, taken from a similar viewpoint, was superimposed so that some idea of the finished appearance could be formed. The prominent tower was never built and, by most people, was not thought to be any great loss.

of rooms or showcases, to make a central meeting place for buyers.'

The architect employed for the development of the site was Harvey W. Corbett, who had already worked for Bush in New York. He produced a scheme which included a 150 ft tower, and some of the drawings were reproduced in the American Architect in 1921. The scheme was given wide coverage in the press, and one of the directors, R.W Peck – but always referred to as 'Bob' of the Bush Company – was responsible for nursing the press for the next sixteen years.

By the time excavation for the foundations actually began in 1920, the plans had beeen modified to build only what is now the Centre Block. There was a flurry of public concern about the prospect of bringing skyscrapers to London, but permission had already been obtained from the London County Council to exceed the prescribed 80 feet for new buildings.

Towards the end of 1921 a slump hit trade and manufacturing. The original purpose of Bush House had to be reconsidered, as the trade activity to maintain Irving Bush's dream no longer existed, and somehow the outlay on the building had to be recouped. The obvious solution was to let out the accommodation as 'high class offices and show rooms' while the other wings of the building were completed, but there was considerable sales resistance to the scheme. The building was considered to be too American, as was the whole area – Kingsway was known as the most American street in London with American firms such as Ingersoll and Kodak based there. Nevertheless the press was soon carrying advertisements for Bush House, and a brochure describing its beauties and facilities was published.

'The architects are Messers. Helmle and Corbett A.I.A of New York. Their aim has been the creation of a modern office and

170

showroom building, combining the best elements from both sides of the Atlantic'. The floors were of 'high class Indian hardwood which can be either polished or left dull, according to the tenants' requirements', while the public areas were clad in Travertine marble. The heating was described as 'modern and unusual' with no 'unsightly and space wasting radiators'. The air itself was heated and 'equable temperature will be maintained… by hot water grilles bedded in the walls at frequent intervals'. Water for the amply distributed lavatories was to be supplied from the Company's own artesian wells. The

combination of such elegance with the convenience of the site would make Bush House one of the most prestigious addresses in London.

Despite the deepening recession during the 1920's and 1930's, the building grew. Centre Block was completed in 1923, the west (now the north-west) wing in 1928. The north-east wing was added by September 1929, the south–east wing by 1930 and the south–west wing by June 1935. This last was let for government offices before completion and was then, and still is, occupied by the Inland Revenue. India House and Melbourne House, not part of Bush House,

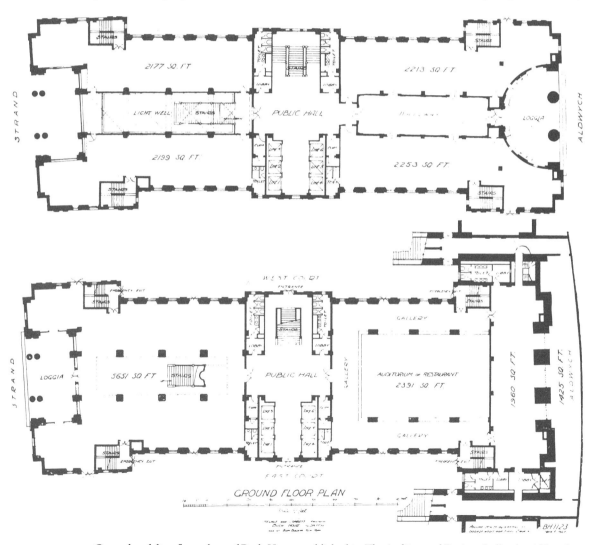

Ground and first-floor plans of Bush House, published in *The Architectural Review*. Sadly, the Aldwych-entrance restaurant no longer exists. It is now a reception area, with the obligatory security guard.

From the prospectus: 'Additional access to the building is gained by six doorways opening on the side courts and roadways. There are no light wells in the building. Every office is a front office looking on to a street.'

were also completed by 1930. The derelict Island site which had been regarded as such an eyesore for so many years had been turned into the series of sweeping, homogenous buildings it is today.

The official opening of Bush House was on July 4th 1925, and the ceremony was performed

by Lord Balfour. The highlight was the unveiling of the two statues symbolising Anglo-American friendship. The sculptor was the American artist Malvina Hoffman, who tells the story of the commission in her autobiography, Yesterday is Tomorrow, *published in 1965:*

'Most of the time spent in the studio during

This accomplished pencil drawing of the proposed Strand entrance to Bush House appeared in the developers' lavish prospectus.

1923, 1924 and 1925 was devoted to the development of a sculptural group to be placed over the entrance of Bush House. Irving T. Bush, who controlled the vast activities of the Bush terminal in Brooklyn, was a curious type of hardhitting businessman and dreamer. He asked me to work with him on his plan to make his building in London a symbol of American and English friendship... The design was to be kept simple, but was to interpret the concept of England and America holding a torch over a Celtic altar with this inscription carved along the base: "Dedicated to the Friendship of English Speaking Peoples."'

173

'The Strand Entrance leads into a large public office on two floors, from which a fine flight of stairs gives access to the main hallway and Aldwych ground level and will form the finest public office in London.'

'A Travertine marble wainscot and classical pilasters carry the eye up to a dignified ceiling.'

'The Aldwych Portico leads to the main staircase through a hallway of imposing dimensions.'

'The building is equipped with four lifts with provision for two more. The lifts are banked in the Central Hall, and will be under the control of an official so as to ensure speedy and comfortable traffic circulation.'

She began by making small models of the group; when these were accepted by the Irving Bush and the architect, quarter-sized models were made, and finally two models, one twelve feet high, another fifteen feet. They were photographed and the enlarged pictures were mounted on three-ply wood, cut out, and set in position on the stone plinth that was to support the group. Malvina wrote:

'...the larger cut-out was set up and "the

boys" looked more in scale with their surroundings. We left them well secured from the back for another day, studying them at different hours, and noted the amazing fact that pedestrians would look up and see the figures and say to one another "Blimey!"'

The statues were carved in sections in New Jersey and shipped to London. They were erected on the plinth eighty feet above the street, having been winched up by a hand–turned

175

windlass and single cable. On one occasion, to Malvina's astonishment, the workmen stopped for a teabreak with a block halfway up, and left it there, promising however to complete the work before they finished for the day. She herself created something of a scandal by insisting on wearing trousers while she worked on finishing the statues high above the ground and, for a short time, became something of a tourist attraction.

The work was finally completed and on the day of the official opening, 'traffic on Kingsway and Aldwych was stopped for half an hour. The crowds gave a cheer, and shivers ran up and down my spine and tears suddenly filled my eyes. It was a thrilling experience.'

Meanwhile Bob Peck's advertising campaign had been successful. By 1925 there were seventeen companies sharing the premises of Bush House, including the London offices of the American newspaper, the Herald Tribune. In 1927 the Parker Pen company moved in, and was to be there until the 1980's. (During this time the cafeteria in the basement was opened, probably the first in London, and customers had to be instructed in how to take a tray, choose their meal and pay the cashier). By the end of 1927 there were nearly a hundred tenants on the eight floors of centre block. The West wing and East wing were listed in 1930, and it was on the East wing that a number of Russian organisations had offices: at different times during the 1930's Bush House saw the arrival and departure of Intourist, the Soviet Steamship Company, the Anglo-Soviet Shipping Company, Arcos (a co-operative trade organisation), representatives of the Russian Commissariat for Heavy Industry, a Russian bookshop and finally

Malvina Hoffman was the sculptor commissioned to provide the stone group to be placed above the Aldwych portico. Here, sections of the group are being assembled at the sculptor's studio in Closter, New Jersey. The top section weighs six tons; the lower, nine tons.

176

– and most ironically of all – Tass. It was not until 1938 when the Air Ministry moved in that all except Intourist moved to Hatton Garden.

Bush House also played a part in the history of the British Secret Service. On the eighth floor of the north-west wing were the offices of C.E. Moore. This name disguised the headquarters of the Z Organisation whose boss was Sir Claude Dansey and whose function was not particularly clear, even to other members of the Secret Service. Its purpose seems mainly to have been 'intelligence gathering', according to the biographers of Sir Claude. Did this extend to the Russians based in the north-east wing of Bush House? The same biographers also say that the BBC world service was in Bush House at the same time; neither BBC archives nor BBC folklore bear this out and, notwithstanding the thirty-year rule, government documents which might shed light are not available.

Bush House was expanding – and Europe was also changing. The beginning of this book tells the story of how the BBC's foreign language broadcasting to Europe began in 1938 from studios in Broadcasting House. It continued there until late 1940, when a landmine was dropped in Portland Place. The whole operation was then transferred to a vacant ice rink in Maida Vale, where the accommodation was very unpopular. There were not enough desks, recording facilities were inadequate and space was cramped. Noel Newsome, soon to become Director of European Broadcasting, was horrified to discover:

'Several hundreds of men and women engaged on the important task of radio propa-

Perched eighty feet above street-level, Malvina Hoffman gives some finishing touches to 'England'.

The moment of unveiling; the group is dedicated 'To the Friendship of English Speaking Peoples'.

179

1929 saw the building of the north-east wing.
This advertisement appeared in *The Times*.

ganda to Europe herded together, at the height of
the blitz, in a former ice-rink with a glass roof
and no air raid shelters at all. The hall had been
partitioned into tiny offices and we were packed
into these like cattle in a market which might at
any moment become a slaughterhouse.'

A new home was found in Bush House
where the studios of J. Walter Thompson,
advertising agents, became available at a rent of
'rather less than £30 per week'. The European
Service moved into Bush House in early 1941,
but found their new premises only slightly
preferable to the ice rink in Maida Vale.

It was not long before questions were being
asked in the House of Commons about the
'Black Hole of Tooting Bec' – the war code

reference to the BBC at Bush House.

During the early part of the Second World
War, Bush House had suffered little bomb
damage – which is perhaps surprising, as the
Luftwaffe must have known of its existence. It
was not until 1944 when a flying bomb landed
on the Aldwych site that there was any
substantial damage. One of the casualties was
the statue representing America – one of
Malvina Hoffman's 'boys' – which lost its left
arm. So he remained until the middle 1970's,
when an American visiting his daughter at the
London School of Economics saw the damaged
statue. He worked for the Indiana Limestone
Company and persuaded the company to send a
new arm, and a stonemason to attach it, in time
for the Silver Jubilee celebrations of Elizabeth II
in 1977.

Over the years Bush House was gradually
invaded by the entire BBC foreign language
services, penetrating each wing in turn. Would
Irving T. Bush have ever achieved such fame for
the building? It seems doubtful, although it is
pleasant to think that his dream of a building
dedicated to 'the Friendship of the English-
speaking Peoples' has been realised in a more
far-reaching and extraordinary way than he
could have ever imagined. However, the BBC
has never owned the building. Its owners have
variously included the Church of Wales, the
Post Office Staff Superannuation Fund and,
now, a Japanese-owned organisation. Its future
as the home of the BBC World Service is
insecure.

Yet Bush House remains embedded in our
perceptions as a BBC building as much as
Broadcasting House or the Televison Centre,
and to millions of overseas listeners it is still the
only building the BBC has.

From *The Architectural Review*, an elevation
drawing of the Strand entrance to Bush House.

A BBC microphone high in the clocktower records the chimes of Big Ben for transmission around the world.

BIBLIOGRAPHY

I have quoted from a number of books in the preceding pages. Those of most interest for anybody who wants to follow the subject further are as follows:

The History of Broadcasting in the United Kingdom, by Asa Briggs (Oxford University Press). Four volumes, published between 1961 and 1979. I have drawn on them for the early years of the BBC. Volume Three, *The War of Words*, deals with the wartime period.

Let Truth be Told, by Gerard Mansell (Weidenfeld and Nicolson, 1982). Written by a former managing director , this is an authoritative history from the opening of the Empire Service to the seventies. The first part of the period is covered in considerable detail, the last two decades rather more briefly.

Truth Betrayed, by W.J. West (Duckworth 1987). This provides an alternative version of the start of the foreign language services, arguing that they were not as independent of the Foreign Office as later BBC accounts have maintained. Its tone is anti-BBC (as it was, not as it is now) and it covers a number of disparate topics, related only in the sense that they are about broadcasing in the thirties.

Conversations with the World, by John Tusa (BBC Books, 1990). This is a compilation of talks about the World Service by the man who became its managing director in 1986. They cover a wide range, including some of the episodes mentioned in this book.

A World in Your Ear, by John Tusa (Broadside Books, 1992). A challenging collection of essays and travel pieces, in which John Tusa reflects on his six years as managing director, during a period of world upheavals.

Media Diplomacy, by Yoel Cohen (Frank Cass and Company, 1986). An account of the relationship between the FCO and the media, including the BBC, this book explores an area which has not been documented in detail before. However, its references to the World Service are not always correct.

BBC Handbooks, issued annually and, in some previous years, called *Yearbooks*, always have a section on the World Service with a good deal of statistical information.

Nation to Nation (World Service Publicity 1991). This is the official account of the work of the World Service in the form of a well-produced booklet. There is also a video with the same title, produced in 1990.

Several language services produced their own histories, usually to mark their 50th anniversaries which in most cases fell in the late 80s or early 90s. One which achieved more than local distribution was *Arab Voices, The BBC Arabic Service 1938-88*, by Peter Partner (BBC, 1988).

*The control room in 1943 during a broadcast of
the 'London Calling Europe' programme.*

INDEX

PICTURE CREDITS

Endpapers   John Robertson
13   The Hulton Picture Library
15   "   "   "   "
16   GEC Marconi
19   John Frost Newspaper Library
20   The Hulton Picture Company
22/3 GEC Marconi
27   John Frost Newspaper Library
28   Popperfoto
31   The Hulton Picture Library
32   BBC Photographic Library
34   The Hulton Picture Company
37   Popperfoto
38   BBC Photographic Library
40   "   "   "
41   Punch Magazine
42   The Hulton Picture Company
45   "   "   "   "
52   BBC Photographic Library
55   BBC Photographic Library
56   Popperfoto
58   BBC Photographic Library
61   The Hulton Picture Company
62   "   "   "   "
64   "   "   "   "
67   "   "   "   "
73   BBC Photographic Library
76-7 Popperfoto
78   "
83   John Frost Picture Library
84   Popperfoto
85   "
89   "
90   BBC Photographic Library
93   The Hulton Picture Company
94   Popperfoto
98   BBC Photographic Library
100   "   "   "
102   Bush House Publicity Department
104   International Broadcasting and Audience
        Research
109   "   "   "   "   "
111   Bush House Publicity Department
112   "   "   "   "
117   Popperfoto
120   Elizabeth Blunt

121   Elizabeth Blunt
122   Dorothy Grenfell-Williams
124   Bush House Publicity Department
126   Popperfoto
127   Bush House Publicity Department
131   Popperfoto
132   "
136   "
137   "
138   Bush House Publicity Department
141   Ian Richardson/Bush House Publicity
        Department
144   Harold Briley
145   Popperfoto
150   Bush House Publicity Department
151   "   "   "   "
152   Ariel Magazine
153   BBC World Service Television Publicity
154   "   "   "   "   "
155   "   "   "   "   "
157   Bush House Publicity Department
158   "   "   "   "
159   "   "   "   "
160   "   "   "   "
161   "   "   "   "
163   "   "   "   "
164   Popperfoto
167   Architectural Review
169   "   "
170   "   "
171   "   "
181   "   "
183   BBC Photographic Library
189   The Hulton Picture Company

Cover photograph: Fred Dick / Bush House
Publicity Department

The Douglas Kennedy anecdote on p.127
appears by kind permission of the *Mail on Sunday* /
Solo Syndication and Literary Agency Ltd.

The Publishers have made every effort to trace copyright holders for the pictures used in this book and
apologise if copyright has been infringed.